The Classic Point of View

THE CLASSIC POINT OF VIEW

Plate 1.—"The Sower," by Jean François Millet.
In the Metropolitan Museum of Art. Vanderbilt Collection.

THE CLASSIC POINT OF VIEW

SIX LECTURES ON PAINTING

DELIVERED ON THE SCAMMON FOUNDATION AT
THE ART INSTITUTE OF CHICAGO
IN THE YEAR 1911

BY

KENYON COX

WITH THIRTY-TWO ILLUSTRATIONS

CHARLES SCRIBNER'S SONS
NEW YORK ❧ ❧ ❧ ❧ MCMXI

Published September, 1911

PREFACE

IN the course of a life devoted to the study, the practice, and the teaching of the art of painting I have, naturally, arrived at some pretty definite conclusions as to the nature of that art and of the problems involved in it—some decided opinions as to what that art has been, is, and should be. These opinions I have tried, however imperfectly, to exemplify in my work and to inculcate in my teaching. They have also, inevitably, colored what I have written. But what I have written has, hitherto, been casual and occasional—a discussion of this or that master, a criticism of this or that particular work of art—and the bases of my criticism, the fundamental ideas on which it is founded, have had, for the most part, to be taken for granted, or to be cursorily and incompletely expressed. These papers have, moreover, been written at long intervals, and for different purposes, and could hardly be entirely consistent with each other. Something like a general point of view could, perhaps, be inferred from them, and something like a consistent body of doctrine made out, by the exercise of sufficient care and sufficient intelligence; but such careful and intelligent consideration as would be necessary could hardly be expected of many readers.

I have therefore welcomed the opportunity afforded by the

invitation from The Art Institute of Chicago to deliver the Scammon Lectures for 1911 to draw up a definitive *credo*—a detailed and explicit confession of artistic faith. The following pages will, accordingly, be found to contain a statement, as clear as I can make it, of what one painter believes and hopes and fears with regard to painting; of what he takes to be the malady of modern art, and of where he looks for the remedy for it. It would be little less than miraculous if such a statement of belief should contain the truth, the whole truth, and nothing but the truth. It must contain errors, and may contain wrongheadedness. At least it is an honest attempt at a contribution to the truth.

It has been said that the criticism of art by an artist is never anything else than an apology for his own work. This is so far true that the expression of opinions definitely held must be the expression of ideals consciously striven for, but I should be sorry to have it thought that my description of what painting should be is intended for a description of what I suppose my own painting to be. We moderns are all in the same boat together. We are all lamentably ill educated, and we are all trying to make up for the faults of our education by strenuous endeavor. We paint as we can, and none of us can afford to have the validity of his opinions judged by his success in carrying them into practice.

KENYON COX.

CONTENTS

ILLUSTRATIONS

ILLUSTRATIONS

[x]

ILLUSTRATIONS

[xi]

THE
CLASSIC POINT OF VIEW

I

THE CLASSIC SPIRIT

THE audience I hope to reach is made up of two parts: of those young artists who have, to some extent, the future of American art in their hands, and of that general public whose influence upon our art, exercised through its patronage and appreciation or its refusal of patronage and appreciation, must be no less real though less direct. In trying to express such opinions and beliefs as are the result of thirty years' practice and study of the art of painting I shall try to remember the general public in the manner of what I have to say, avoiding technical jargon and striving to speak in the language of all the world. But it is to the young artists that I would especially appeal; first, because it is more important that they should be right; second, because there is more danger that they will go wrong.

The public is in little danger. In general, it is too conservative rather than the reverse. It listens, in a bewildered way, to the hurly-burly of conflicting schools and movements, tries to believe in the latest discovery of the newest newspaper critic, shrugs its shoulders, and buys an old-fashioned picture that it can understand. It may neglect true genius but it gives little active encouragement to the sham. The young artist is more easily led astray by false lights. He sees countless experiments, hears countless doctrines and theories, listens to the exaltation of incompetence or eccentricity and to the poohpoohing of all quiet attainment. The more ardent he is the more difficult he finds it to keep his head. Why should he toil and make slow progress toward an unattainable goal when so many short cuts to notoriety, if not to fame, are opened before him? Quick! let him get something before the public. It is much easier to find a new way of being bad than to master the old way of being good, and the new bad thing is, at any rate, sure to be noticed. I protest, it is wonderful to me that there should any longer be such a thing as a student of art, it has become so easy to be hailed a master.

That there are serious students, however, the existence of a few of our schools of art sufficiently testifies; and it is to the serious students of to-day, the serious artists of to-morrow, that I especially make my plea for the Classic Spirit.

The Classic Spirit is the disinterested search for perfection; it is the love of clearness and reasonableness and self-control; it is, above all, the love of permanence and

of continuity. It asks of a work of art, not
that it shall be novel or effective, but that
it shall be fine and noble. It seeks not
merely to express individuality or emotion
but to express disciplined emotion and
individuality restrained by law. It strives
for the essential rather than the accidental,
the eternal rather than the momentary—
loves impersonality more than personality,
and feels more power in the orderly succession of the hours and the seasons than
in the violence of earthquake or of storm.
And it loves to steep itself in tradition. It
would have each new work connect itself
in the mind of him who sees it with all the
noble and lovely works of the past, bringing them to his memory and making their
beauty and charm a part of the beauty and
charm of the work before him. It does not
deny originality and individuality—they
are as welcome as inevitable. It does not
consider tradition as immutable or set
rigid bounds to invention. But it desires

that each new presentation of truth and beauty shall show us the old truth and the old beauty, seen only from a different angle and colored by a different medium. It wishes to add link by link to the chain of tradition, but it does not wish to break the chain.

The Classic Spirit, as I understand it, and wish to present it to you, has little to do with the so-called "classic school" founded by Jacques Louis David. Indeed this spirit seldom was lacking in the art of the world before his advent. Until the end of the eighteenth century the stream of tradition in the art of painting was continuous, and even the most powerful individualities and the most romantic temperaments stood but little aside from it. Michelangelo himself, the greatest of romanticists, was a classic by one side of his nature, and it was only that side that was understood by his contemporaries or was effective with them; and even Rembrandt, strangely and imperiously as he modified what he found there, searched the art of the past for the foundations of his own. These were the exceptions. The others, even the greatest, were content to modify slightly the tradition they had received and to hand it down to their successors. Giorgione and Titian enriched and broadened the tradition they had received from Bellini; Rubens studied their method, founded his own upon it, and in his turn passed it on to Watteau and the eighteenth century.

Then came the French Revolution, and among the many things, good and bad, for which it is responsible, one is the breaking short off of the traditions of painting. David, a revolutionary in art as in politics, influenced by the imagined revival of Roman ideals, invented an art founded on antique sculpture—an art which contemned color, neglected light and shade, destroyed technical beauty, and reduced even drawing to a kind of mechanical correctness without life or accent—and by his powerful character and great influence imposed this art upon all continental Europe. When the storm was over it was only in the one country which had continuously stood out against the revolution —it was only in England—that any vestiges of the art of painting remained. Prudhon, who had remained a real painter in spite of David, died in 1823, and Gros, who would have been a real painter if he could, committed suicide. France was given over to the Guérins and Girodets, and in Germany they were producing cartoons. Lawrence, with his clever but meretricious echoes of Reynolds and Gainsborough, and Constable, the preserver of the landscape tradition, were the only painters left.

Then began the long confusion of cross currents and opposing forces which is the history of modern art. For the first time since art began there was no accepted tradition, no authoritative guide; it was every man for himself. The system of apprenticeship, by which a painter learned to practise his art in a recognized and approved manner before making such changes in that manner as his own temperament and his own needs might suggest, was gone; and if it could have been revived there were no longer any masters to take apprentices. The school, which had succeeded to this system, taught only a little drawing, and that of a purely naturalistic kind. Before each individual artist, for the last hundred years, there has been the impossible and heart-breaking task of creating his art again from the beginning; of finding out both what he wanted to do and how he should do it; of discovering and piecing together from the study of nature and of the art of the past, composition and drawing, light and shade and color, even the nature of his

Plate 2.—"The Testament of Endamidas," by Nicolas Poussin.

In the Collection of Count Moltke, at Copenhagen.

materials and the method of handling them. Is it any wonder that modern art has produced great talents but very few masters? Is it any wonder that we can show nothing like the assured and abundant production of the giants of the past? Is it any wonder that the record of modern artists is so often that of failure and despair; of modern art that of inconclusive gropings, leading nowhere but into the bog?

What has been generally known as the Romantic Revolution in art was, so far at least as painting is concerned, essentially an effort to get back the traditions which had been lost, to renew the connection with the past, to rediscover the art. Its great leader, Delacroix, was a man of ardent and romantic temperament, but he had a great respect for the past and for tradition, and it was a sound instinct that led him to found his art upon that of Rubens, the heir of the Venetians and the modifier of their manner to suit more modern requirements. From Rubens, through Watteau, was descended the whole of the French eighteenth century, and from Rubens, through Van Dyck, the whole English School, then still subsisting, though its greatest days were past. If the old conditions could be restored at all it would be by beginning again with the great Fleming as the nearest source of authentic tradition. In a splendid effort to do this Delacroix spent his life, and he produced many noble works in the course of it, but in spite of such personal successes, that life was, in the main, a failure. He was praised and admired and made a member of the Institute, but he could not found a school with a stable tradition.

A similar attempt was made by the great landscape painters, Rousseau and Corot. They were both profound students of nature, and the addition they made to the world's stock of knowledge of natural aspects was so great that we are apt to think of them as naturalists first of all. In reality they were both of classic temper. Rousseau founded his art upon Ruysdael and Hobbema, Corot founded his upon Claude and Poussin. Their effort was to vitalize tradition and turn it to new uses; to gain new knowledge but to crystallize it in forms reminiscent of the past. Look at any of their characteristic works and you will feel, underlying the detailed study of natural forms in Rousseau, underlying the atmospheric mystery of Corot, a something which connects these modern pictures with everything fine that had been done before them. Modern as they are, they are pervaded with the Classic Spirit.

But of all these "revolutionaries" the most classically minded was precisely that one who was considered the most revolutionary of all, Jean François Millet. This "man of the woods," as his fellow pupils in Delaroche's studio called him, this

painter of peasants whom the critics of the
day thought a socialist and almost a bomb
thrower, was a conservative of conserva-
tives, a worshipper of that stern old classicist Poussin, the last practitioner of
"the grand style." So essentially classic
was he that, in the pages to follow, you
will find me citing him more often, in illustration of my meaning, than any other
modern painter, unless it be that greatest
of the upholders of the official school—
Ingres.

For, during all the changes that have
passed over the art of France, the "school"
has subsisted, and still subsists, modifying
slowly its regimen, producing many re-
spectable painters if very few great ones,
supplying a training most imperfect, indeed, but the only thing resembling a
training of any kind that is to be had. To
the school the very men who have revolted
against it owe a great part of their effective force, and to the school, as a restrain-

ing influence, we probably owe it that the present state of the art is not more chaotic and more hopeless than it actually is.

Of the destructive and disintegrating influences that have been brought to bear on modern art, the most damaging was probably the invention of photography. In the old days the young artist learned his art first, accepting the methods and the formulæ of his master, before he went to nature that he might add his own observations to the inherited stock. Nowadays he is set to study nature in the beginning, being left to find his own conventions as best he may. The result of this has been greatly to increase the tendency of the young artist to consider the exact imitation of nature as the primary problem of art. Photography seemed to show him, all at once, what nature actually looks like, and painting embarked on a long and ruinous emulation of the camera. What had been a natural and, in some respects, a healthy and necessary pre-occupation of the student became the guiding principle of a lifetime, and men thought not of how to produce a beautiful picture, but of what were the exact facts of the world about them.

In England the result was the Pre-Raphaelite movement, which finally transformed itself into the æsthetic movement of Rossetti and Burne-Jones, but not before it had destroyed what was left of the older English school. Some part of the old tradition still lingered there, and Etty, though an artist of limited range, was a sound and brilliant technician. He has had no successor, and English art, since the days of the Brotherhood, has been drifting rudderless, like that of other countries.

In France the same desire for realism influenced a long line of men, from Courbet, who, fortunately for us, was not so realistic as he thought himself, to Bastien-Le

Page. I was myself a student in Paris
when Bastien was making some of his first
great successes, and can look back, now,
with a certain amusement, at the exaggerated estimation in which we held him.
Here, it seemed to us, was the last word of
art—the consummation to which everything had been tending. All progress in
art had been, we thought, a nearer approximation to the truth of nature—here
was the truth itself, as literal and as like as
the image at the back of a camera. The
exact portraiture of a particular peasant
woman in a particular hay-field under the
nearly unchanging light of a cloudy sky—
that being the only outdoor light in which
such detailed portraiture is possible—
what more could one ask? Well, somehow,
one did ask more. Composition and line
and color and beauty of workmanship
continued to assert themselves as desirable
qualities, and by this time all the world is
pretty well agreed that pure naturalism is

a failure. Now that some artists and some critics are trying to prove that photography may be an art we are ready for the definite conclusion that art should not be photographic.

Another manifestation of the naturalistic tendency is what has usually been called the impressionistic movement—that which people are now beginning to call luminism. What is essential in it is an investigation of the laws of light and an effort to invent means of rendering the effects of natural light upon objects. It is not necessary, here, to go deeply into the question of the nature or validity of these means, or the measure of success attained. The impressionists managed, at least, to call attention to the existence of light and color and to enliven the palette even of the schoolmen. But the movement was scientific rather than artistic, and the pictures of its strongest man, Claude Monet, often seem like a series of demonstrations rather

Plate 3.—"Une Veuve," from the painting by Alfred Stevens.

In the Collection of Mr. Martin A. Ryerson, Chicago.

than things of beauty created for human delight. It is, really, only in this country that the impressionistic formula has been seized upon for its capabilities of beauty and, in the hands of Hassam and others, bent to the ends of decoration.

While all this intensive study of natural fact and natural aspect was going on, there were artists who revolted from it; artists who cared more for art than for nature and whose effort was for self-expression rather than for the recording of observations. I shall mention but two of them, men of widely differing temperaments and achievements, because the nature and the degree of their success and failure seem to me symptomatic of the disease of nineteenth century art—Gustave Moreau and James MacNeill Whistler. Moreau was a man of intellect, a poet and a dreamer; Whistler was pure painter, caring only for the material beauty of his production, and despising any literary implication.

Both were entirely out of sympathy with the art that was practised about them and with the public to whom they must appeal. Moreau shut himself up and produced in loneliness and isolation a series of strange works, often of great beauty but with a taint of morbidity in them. Whistler fought the world instead of flying from it, and wasted in brilliant but futile controversy half the strength that should have gone to the creation of masterpieces. The weakness of the one was a lack of balance, of the other a lack of training; of both, the absence of any normal and right relation to their public. How pitifully slight is the production of either compared to the magnificent fecundity of those old masters who, secure in the possession of a sound tradition and assured of a constant demand for what they could do, poured forth masterpiece after masterpiece with the ease of a fruit tree bearing good fruit. For it is only in our modern time that the unpopularity of the greatest artists has become so proverbial that we are tempted to think unpopularity a proof of greatness. In the great days of art the artist understood his public and his public understood him, and together they produced those works which we still admire. It is not till the time of Rembrandt that we hear of unappreciated genius, and even then Rembrandt is the exception, not the rule.

It is this lack of relation between the artist and the public that has created the modern exhibition, and the exhibition, necessary as it has become, is a necessary evil. It has made art, what it should never be, competitive, and has set each artist to outshriek his rivals in the bid for public notice. First it created those bastard forms of art, the "gallery picture" and the "machine du Salon." Then it begat the sensational subject, and we had blood and horror as our daily diet. When these became too common to attract attention there was nothing left for it but eccentricity of method; and that eccentricity has become more and more extreme until it has seemed that modern art is bent upon emulation of the Gadarene swine and is rushing down a steep place into the sea.

Of some of the phases of ultra-modern art I find it difficult to speak with fairness or with any patience. I should wish to believe in a certain element of honest conviction in it and to accept the explanation of its adherents that it is a revolt against naturalism and an effort to get back the abstract quality and expressiveness of lines and colors, independently of their representative character. If so, the pendulum has swung as far to one side as it had swung to the other. But there seems to me, also, to be a vast amount of mere charlatanism among the Neo-Impressionists and the Post-Impressionists, and an even larger amount of sheer madness. Van Gogh cut off his own ear when he failed

to kill his friend Gauguin with a razor;
Toulouse-Lautrec had a keeper; several
others committed suicide or died in asy-
lums. And still the game goes on, until we
have men painting and exhibiting things
made up of outlines that look like the
drawings of a bad boy on the walls of an
outhouse and of flat masses of primary
colors arranged with no conceivable relation to nature. We have even had compositions in which the human figure is
represented by a series of triangles and a
portrait is symbolized by an arrangement
of cubes, and we have critics writing
books and articles to prove that this is the
real and vital art, the "art of the future."

It seems to me quite evident that any
further "progress" in this direction is impossible. We have reached the edge of the
cliff and must turn back or fall into the
abyss. It may be that such a turning back
is impossible. It may be that there is never
again to be a sane and vigorous art, firmly

based on a sound tradition, appealing to and understood by its public and producing naturally and without convulsion something for which that public has a use. But if such an art *is* to exist again it can only be by the reversal of those tendencies that have brought us to the present pass. The scientific spirit, the contempt of tradition, the lack of discipline and the exaltation of the individual have very nearly made an end of art. It can only be restored by the love of beauty, the reverence for tradition, the submission to discipline and the rigor of self-control. We must get back to the permanent and the eternal—we must regain the Classic Spirit.

This spirit has much more in common with modern naturalism than with modern emotionalism and modern individualism, though it is apart from either. It can make room—has always made room—for the study of nature. It recognizes that painting is essentially an imitative art, and that its raw material is the aspect of the external world. It can use any amount of knowledge of this aspect, and it has no toleration of ignorance or indolence; but it also recognizes that painting is an art, not a science, and that knowledge un-assimilated and unsubdued to the ruling purpose of art is useless and obstructive. The primary business of painting is to create a beautiful surface, beautifully divided into interesting shapes, enlivened with noble lines, varied with lovely and harmonious colors. Its secondary business is to remind the spectator of things he has seen and admired in nature, and to create the illusion of truth. The amount of actual truth it shall contain will vary with the purpose and the situation. Very little will do for the ornamentation of a vase, but an easel-picture may contain so much as to seem—not to be—an exact record of observed facts. If it break the connection altogether and cease to suggest nature it may still be art but it will cease to be the art of painting. On the other hand, the amount of art it shall contain is constant. The artistic intention must dominate everything, control everything, mould everything to its purpose. Its sovereignty must be absolute and complete.

But so to control facts, and to bend them to one's purpose, one must know them, and know them vastly better than he who merely copies them. There is a certain kind of naturalism that is only less indolent than the ignoring of nature. With a good eye and a good deal of practice you may copy a head or an arm, pretty well, without much intellectual strain. To *learn* that head or that arm, so that you shall be able to distinguish the essential from the accidental; so that you shall know what is important in it, and to your purpose, and what is not; to master it, in a word— that is a man's work and takes the whole of the man.

Photograph by A. Giraudon.

Plate 4.—"The Punished Son," by Greuze.

In the Louvre.

But if it is difficult to learn nature, as a classicist should know it, it is even more difficult to learn art. It is not merely that we have, to-day, no authoritative tradition, and must build one for ourselves. If we, in this country, were entirely shut off from the rest of the world and from all the art that has been produced, we should, quite naturally, set to work to produce an art of our own, and we should produce it. It might take a long time in the doing, but we should do it, as every other people has done. That sort of natural production has, however, become forever impossible. Photography and modern means of communication have brought the ends of the earth together and rendered all ages contemporary. We have become as familiar with the art of Egypt and of Assyria as with that of the nineteenth century, and the art of Japan is no more strange to us than that of England. We know all art, superficially—we know no art thoroughly.

We have all the traditions to study, and we have none of our own. We can but pick and choose, trying to disentangle the important and the universal from the unimportant and the local or temporary, to decide what is proper and useful for us and to neglect the rest. We can only hope to make a tradition for ourselves out of many traditions by a series of eliminations.

The task is a tremendous one and, as I have said, I do not know whether it is possible of performance. But there are reasons which lead me to believe that if the thing can be done at all it is more likely to be done here in America than anywhere else.

Because we are a new people the world seems to expect of us a new art, radically different in some strange way from the art of older countries, and to be disappointed at our conservatism. It seems to me that precisely because we are a new people our art might have been expected to be conservative. We have not yet had enough of the old and fine things to be wearied of them. We do not find it necessary to strain our invention in the effort to discover some new spice for a jaded appetite. In this country it is only a few critics who suffer from artistic indigestion —the rest of the world is not yet tired of hearing Aristides called the Just. We are, in all things, at bottom, a conservative people, but in nothing are we so much so as in all matters concerning art. Our literature, our architecture, our painting and sculpture are more conservative and less influenced by fads and fashions than any now going in the world. Of our great public buildings it may be said, and it has been made a reproach to them, that there is nothing distinctively American about them. Yet such buildings are produced nowhere else, to-day, because everywhere else, architects are striving to produce something new. Here they are willing to do the obvious—the classic—thing because the classic thing has not yet become obvious to us. If we go on doing the classic thing in architecture until its language has become natural and easy to us, there is a possibility that we may begin to use it originally, and to produce, almost without knowing it, a national style. If we strive for originality now, there is little hope of anything better than the architectural chaos that we have had so much of.

As with our architecture, so it is with our painting. There is, already, something like an "American School" of painting, and the most notable characteristic of that school is its conservatism. It is by no means so conservative as I would have it, or so free from the dangers which threaten all modern art, but it is, on the whole, the sanest and soundest school existing.

I have heard this conservatism of our American artists attributed to a mere desire of popularity, rather than to anything like a respect for law and for tradition on the part of the artists themselves. If this were true there would still be something to be said in favor of it. The public is entirely right if it demands sanity and sobriety of the artist; and the artist is entirely right if, without compromising his artistic ideal, he strives to produce something which the public wants. After all, why should not art be popular? The greatest art always has been so. The art of Phidias was popular in Athens; the art of Titian was popular in Venice; the art of Raphael was popular in Rome and everywhere else, and has remained popular to this day. Under proper conditions art would always be popular, for the artist would be one of the people, having the same ideals and thoughts and feelings as the public he served, and would, quite naturally, express the mind of his public as his public would have it expressed. I do not say that all great art is popular—

still less that all popular art is great. But I do say that when art is not popular something is wrong, either with the art or with the public—or with both. And when inferior art is popular it is because of the good in it, not because of the evil.

But it is not true that the mere desire of popularity—the commercial consideration of what will sell—is at the bottom of the comparative conservatism of American painting. American painters are as sincere and as earnest as any in the world, but their sincerity and their earnestness are not leading them to the search for novelty. In all countries the ordinary painter, like the ordinary man of any kind, takes the easiest way. The mass of the painters of this country, as of all countries, practise the current methods of the time; but the exceptional men, instead of striving for something new, are trying to get back to something old. They are trying to get back composition and the monumental style; they are trying to get back the expressiveness of the line; they are attempting purity and beauty of color; they are even trying to revive old technical methods, underpainting in tempera and using glazes again, which modern art had almost tabooed.

I would not have you think there is little to be done—if it were so I should not be making this plea for the Classic Spirit. There is very much to be done. Our art is not only far below what an art should be; not only far below what the art of the Renaissance was; it is still far below what the art of France was in the earlier part of the nineteenth century. But just as certainly, I believe, is it the best art now being produced in the world, and the art, of all now being produced in the world, that has the most in common with the great art of the past and the largest promise for the art of the future.

In the course of a trip to Europe, taken last summer, the truth of this statement was strongly impressed upon me. It is true I saw little of modern painting, and it was the study of older art that made me feel the kinship to it of the art we are making here. The more I saw of the great masterpieces of the Renaissance the more encouraged I felt as to the validity of the best work I had seen at home, and the more I found myself saying, "This is what we, in America, have been trying to do." For the other end of the comparison I must call another witness—one out of many. Last spring a very distinguished American painter who has resided for many years in France was temporarily in this country, and was taken by a brother artist to see the exhibitions of the Ten American Painters and of the National Academy of Design. The exhibition of the Academy was, as it always is, crowded and ill-displayed from lack of adequate

Plate 5.—"The Contract," by Hogarth.

In the National Gallery, London; from the series: "Marriage A-la-Mode."

galleries, and this lack of space and crowd-
ing had kept, as it always does, some of
our best artists from exhibiting at all. It
was a fair average display of current work,
not a selection of the best. Yet in the
opinion of this artist, fresh from years of
foreign residence, it was of an extraordinarily high average of merit, which it
would be impossible to parallel, to-day, in
Paris. He was quite as enthusiastic as to
the smaller exhibition, saying again, that
such a showing of ten men would be impossible in Paris; to which the not too
boastful answer was: "We have twenty
others as good, here in America."

There is plenty of such testimony, if it
were necessary to cite it. We do not know
how good our art really is. We are, naturally enough, afraid of our own judgment
and unable to believe that anything can be
really good until the world has said so in
unmistakable terms. To such of the general public as will listen to me I would

say: patronize our own art. Patronize it as discriminatingly and intelligently as possible, but patronize it. There is no other way in which you can do so much good to art, and, if you need a more personal motive, there is no other way in which you are so likely to get your money's worth.

To the young artist my message would be somewhat different. To him I would say: our art is, indeed, the best alive to-day, but the best is but poor compared to what has been or to what should be. Let us strive to make it equal to any, and to that end let us fill ourselves with the Classic Spirit. Let us strive for perfection, recognizing that perfection is only to be attained by discipline and by self-control. Let us think not what is new, but what is good; not what is easy and attractive, but what is eternally right. Let us attach ourselves to what is noblest in the art of the past, trying to understand the reason of its nobility, and spend ourselves in generous emulation. Let us believe that passion and personality will find their way into our art, if we have them, and that it is a poor and sapless individuality that can be killed by a little hard work. Only in this spirit can a great art be created. Only in this spirit can a true school of painting exist. If we have this spirit, I believe, there is at least a chance that a great school of painting may come to exist here in our own country.

II

THE SUBJECT IN ART

THE idea that the subject of a work of art is of no importance whatever has been taught us so thoroughly and has become so ingrained in us that it seems almost necessary to apologize for mentioning such a thing at all to a modern audience. We have been so deeply impressed with the truth—for it is a truth as far as it goes —that it is the amount of art contained in a given picture which counts, not the matter on which that art is expended, that we have concluded that any subject will do as well as any other, and that there are no distinctions of subject matter worth considering. We have so completely learned that a still-life by Chardin may be better than an altar-piece by Carlo Dolci that we have forgotten to ask whether it can be as good as Titian's "Entombment."

One may be quite prepared to admit that the old rigid categories, by which a history painter was always superior to a genre painter and any figure painter was the better of any landscape painter, were a trifle absurd. One may feel that the French Academicians, admitting Watteau to their membership only under the slighting title of "Peintre des Fêtes Galantes," were belittling a greater man than any of themselves. One may welcome the modern conquest of freedom of choice as a salutary victory for common-sense—a victory which was, after all, only a reconquest; for the old masters made no distinctions or specialties, every master being simply a painter, and painting what came his way, from an altar-piece to a signboard. Yet a distinction as to nobility of subject matter will still subsist. Some subjects will permit and demand the exercise of greater powers than others, and are, in so far as they do this, nobler subjects. A man may paint a jug, a loaf of bread and a dish of grapes and may show, in doing so, such delicate perception of gradations of light, such fine sense of color, such mastery of surfaces and textures, above all such a modest and pure spirit, as shall mark him a true artist and make him forever admirable and lovable. But he cannot put into the rendering of such a subject the lofty powers of design and drawing that make the ceiling of the Sistine Chapel one of the wonders of the world. You cannot make a Michelangelo out of a Chardin, and you cannot exert the powers of a Michelangelo on the subjects of Chardin. It may be better to succeed with Chardin than to fail in attempting to be a Michelangelo, but the powers exercised by Michelangelo, and the subjects which permit of the exercise of such powers, are eternally the nobler and the more important.

The modern view was admirably expressed in a favorite saying of the late Augustus Saint-Gaudens which has been frequently quoted. "You may do anything," he used to say, "it is the way you do it that counts." As he meant it, the saying is a true one, for he did not mean that if you do a thing cleverly enough, with great technical skill and command of material, that alone will make it a great work of art. He included sincerity, nobility of temper, high purpose, a love of beauty and a love of truth, among the elements of "the way you do it"; and he would have placed mere virtuosity, however excellent a thing in itself, far below these qualities in his scale of values. He would have been the first to admit that there is a sense in which the reverse of his proposition is equally true. If the thing done be noble it does not matter how it is done. If the picture or the statue have dignity of conception and grandeur of mass and line, if it conveys to you a sense of imaginative grasp on the part of the artist, if it arouses emotion and elevates the mind, it may be ruggedly—almost clumsily—executed; it may be entirely devoid of surface charm and technical dexterity and be none the less a work of the highest art.

It will not be badly executed, for the feeling of the artist, however right and noble, can only be expressed by technical means, and the means used must, necessarily, be right means for the purpose of such expression. If he has conveyed his meaning it is certain that he has sufficiently mastered the language by which such meanings may be conveyed. But it is by what he has said and done that you judge him. How he has said and done it may be a question of great and absorbing interest to other artists and to special students of art, but is, after all,

Plate 6.—"The Surrender of Breda," by Velasquez.

In the Prado.

a subsidiary question to the world for whom he works.

I can think of no better instance of what I mean than the earliest of Jean François Millet's great series of peasant pictures, "The Sower" (Pl. 1), now in the Vanderbilt Collection at the Metropolitan Museum of New York. Before he created it Millet had painted a number of charming little pictures of nude female figures, admirably executed, supremely able in their way, by no means to be despised, but not what he wanted to do—not the expression of his greatest powers. He wanted to paint an Epic of the Soil, and the first book of it was the sowing of the seed. The brilliant technical method of his earlier work was not suited to his present purpose; it was too suave, too rich, too easy, to give the impression of rugged strength and simplicity that he wished to convey. He had to invent a new handling and a new technical manner, which he afterward developed to such perfection that, in his later works, his mere painting is as wonderful as his grand design and powerful drawing. But in this first essay in the new manner he is a little awkward, almost fumbling and clumsy. It does not greatly matter. The largeness of silhouette, the august grandeur of movement, the nobility of conception carry it off. The thing done is fine, and any rudeness in the manner of the doing becomes a matter of little importance.

This may seem like a question of treatment rather than a question of subject, but it is not entirely so. The two things are intimately related. Millet could not have given the same effect of nobility if his subject had not been intrinsically noble. Doubtless so great an artist was able to elevate any subject by the largeness of his treatment and the "three pears on a plate or table" may well have been, for a painter, such a revelation of his power as our own Wyatt Eaton found them. Nevertheless, if Millet had painted nothing but a series of such subjects he would not have been the great master we know, and some of his highest powers would never have been exercised.

The highest subject for the exercise of the greatest powers of a painter is the human figure, nude or so draped as to express, rather than to conceal, its structure and movement—the subject of the Greeks and of Michelangelo—and this is the subject of all Millet's work. After the early days he seldom did an entirely unclothed figure, though his "Goose Girl Bathing" is one of the most wonderful and beautiful things in the world, but it was the nude he was continually striving to express. In the costume of his peasants he found long-used garments taking the form of the body, becoming almost a part of it, as he said to Eaton, and "expressing even more than the nude the larger and simpler forms of nature."

The human figure, its bulk and form and action, that was the subject of all his works, but the more specific subjects of the separate pictures were equally noble and universal. Doubtless the academic makers of categories would not have seen or understood this. They would have classed him as a painter of peasants with Jan Steen or Ostade. But Millet has painted nothing trivial or unimportant, no smokers or card-players, no drinking in taverns or dancing in rings. Every one of his great pictures has a subject as old as mankind, a subject of immense and eternal import to the race. Plowing and sowing and reaping, the hewing of wood and the drawing of water, carding and spinning and the making of garments, things in which all mankind is interested and in which the bulk of mankind always has been and always will be occupied, these are his subjects. Shepherds have watched their sheep from the time before Abraham was, as Millet's shepherds watch theirs, and

mothers have fed their young or assisted
"The First Steps" since the Garden of
Eden. Fortunately for his purpose, the
life of the tillers of the soil had changed
but little and machinery had not yet in-
vaded the fields, and he was able to find in
the daily life of the people about him subjects truly typical of the history of humanity—subjects much more essentially
and eternally classic than the straddling
Greek and Roman warriors of those who
arrogated to themselves the title of classi-
cists.

I would by no means intimate that it is
the duty of every artist to attempt subjects of the highest class. It is rather his
duty to choose such subjects as are suited
to his powers and give greatest scope for
the development of the qualities he possesses. He may paint genre or landscape
or portrait or still-life and be a true artist
whose work the world will cherish, for the
powers necessary to success in any of these

fields are as rare as they are truly admirable. Still, it is not true that all subjects are alike, or that success with one kind of subject is as good ás success with another. One may sincerely admire Frans Hals and be sincerely glad that he painted what he could do so well instead of trying to do that at which he would certainly have failed; one is not therefore, ready to rank him with Michelangelo and above Raphael. One may derive unalloyed pleasure from the marvellous skill of Vollon and yet be certain that the art of Millet is of a higher kind. The different kinds of merit proper to the different kinds of subject can never be quite perfectly united—there must always be some sacrifice, somewhere—but now and then, in the works of the greatest masters, so much of technical beauty and perfection is found united to so much of grandeur of conception and largeness of style that we may receive from one work the largest possible sum of enjoyment. These are the world's unapproachable masterpieces.

But if the modern world has come to think any subject as good as any other it has made one very curious exception to the rule. It has come to think what it calls "the literary subject" an actual drawback, and to consider that the presence, in a work of art, of what is called a "story" is of itself enough to relegate that work to an inferior rank. Yet how such an opinion can have been arrived at, in view of the history of art in all ages, is the greatest of puzzles. For art, from its beginnings among the cave men, has always told stories; and its twin purposes of illustration and of decoration have always gone hand in hand, illustration being generally, in the mind of the artist as in that of his audience, the more important of the two. The Assyrian celebrated the prowess of his kings in hunt or in battle and the Egyptian recorded the whole life of the people upon the walls of royal tombs. The art of Greece told the story of its gods and heroes on every vase and on every temple front, and the pediments of the Parthenon recounted the legends of the birth of Pallas and of the founding of Athens.

In like manner the art of the Renaissance occupied itself, almost exclusively, with the sacred story of the Old and New Testaments or with the legends of the saints, from the time that Giotto painted the life of Francis at Assisi and the life of Christ in the Arena Chapel until Raphael spread his "Bible" upon the vaultings of the Loggia of the Vatican. The greatest work of its mightiest master, the most sublime and awe-inspiring creation of all art, was nothing else than the story of the Creation and the Fall of Man, so told, with such clarity and such power, as never story, before or since, was told in colors. Even the Venetians, those lovers of the sumptuous and the decorative, the crea-

Plate 7.—"Washington Laying Down his Commission," by E. H. Blashfield.

In the Baltimore Court House.

tors of what we know as genre, could not get on without a story to tell, and when the story seems absent to us it is because it has been lost, not because it was not there. Titian's enigmatic picture which is traditionally known as the "Sacred and Profane Love" is now said to represent "Medea and Venus," and Giorgione's "Partie Champêtre" and "Soldier and Gypsy" are thought to be illustrations of this or that Italian novel.

It may be that in these later instances the story was a concession to the demands of the public, and that while the ostensible subject was the temptation of Medea by Venus the real subject was the contrast between a nude figure and a draped one. It may be that Giorgione would have been equally content with his idyllic dreams had they no definite context in his mind or in the minds of those for whom he painted. It certainly was not so with the earlier masters, and as certainly it was not so with

that later master, Rembrandt. It is a commonplace of criticism that Dutch art told
no stories, and that the Dutch burghers,
for whom it was created, asked nothing of
it but the portraiture of themselves and
their wives or of their daily life and their
tame and comfortable country. The artist
who attempted more did so at his peril,
and Ruysdael paid for his love of rocks
and waterfalls as Rembrandt paid for his
love of stories, with poverty and discour-
agement. Yet Rembrandt was always telling stories. His public did not want them;
it wanted nothing of him but portraits that
should be like; and when his portraits
ceased to be neat and obvious likenesses it
wanted nothing of him whatever. Yet he
painted stories over and over again, his
etchings are filled with stories, and, more
than all, his drawings, which the public
never saw, are one long series of illustrations. He was haunted with stories from
which he could not escape and to which

he returned again and again, illustrating
their every phase and turning and twist-
ing them in every aspect. There is the
story of Lot, the story of Joseph, the story
of Tobit, for each of which he made almost numberless drawings, and the story
of Christ, which is the subject of his greatest etchings. He was a great painter, a
great master of light and shade, a portrait
painter who has excelled all others in the
rendering of the human soul behind the
features; but more than anything else he
was a great story-teller, and his imaginative grasp of a story and his power of so
telling it that it shall seem real and imme-
diate to us, as if it had actually happened
before our very eyes, is perhaps the most
wonderful of his many wonderful gifts.

So great has been the dominance of the
story in art that even the landscape painters of the seventeenth century, to whose
main purpose story-telling was in no way
necessary, nearly always put in a few fig-

ures supposed to represent the characters in some legend, sacred or profane; and the light and frivolous art of the eighteenth century tells stories too, though the stories may be as light and frivolous as the manner of telling.

But if you wish to know how seriously the telling of the story may be taken by a great artist you must read the fragments of criticism left us by that great nineteenth century classicist, Jean François Millet. In his letters, in the fragments of his conversation recorded for us by others, in his few formal announcements of his beliefs about art, you will find hardly anything else mentioned. For all he says about them, such things as drawing, or color, or the handling of his material, might as well not exist. Apparently his whole mind is concentrated on the story of the picture and the manner of its telling—everything else is of value only as it helps the clarity and force of the expression. For him "Art is a language and . . . all language is intended for the expression of ideas." "The artist's first task is to find an arrangement that will give full and striking expression to his idea." And again, "To have painted things that mean nothing is to have borne no fruit." Hear him discoursing on a print, after his favorite master Poussin, of a man upon his death-bed (Pl. 2): "How simple and austere the interior; only that which is necessary, no more; the grief of the family, how abject; the calm movement of the physician as he lays the back of his hand upon the dying man's heart; and the dying man, the care and sorrow in his face, and his hands . . . they show age, toil, and suffering." Not one word about anything else—all other things are but means—the telling of the story is the end and the essential. He has given us, in a letter to a critic of art, a more formal profession of faith—a brief statement of what he thought fundamental in art and of the principles by which he was consciously guided in his own work.

"The objects introduced in a picture," he says, "should not appear to be brought together by chance, and for the occasion, but should have a necessary and indispensable connection. I want the people that I represent to look as if they belonged to their place, and as if it would be impossible for them to think of being anything else but what they are. A work must be all of a piece, and persons and objects must always be there for a purpose. I wish to say fully and forcibly what is necessary, so much so that I think things feebly said had better not be said at all, since they are, as it were, spoilt and robbed of their charm. But I have the greatest horror of useless accessories, however brilliant they may be. These things only serve to distract and weaken the general effect."

The Classic Spirit, in its austerest form, as it envisages the subject and its treatment, could not be more clearly expressed; and Millet's practice was strictly in accord with his theories. His pictures are seldom so specifically related to a written text as are those of Rembrandt, but each of his characters has a history and a station, and "could never think of being other than what it is." One of his very great works is "The Woman Carrying Water," which hangs beside "The Sower" in the Metropolitan Museum. Of its purely artistic merits I may have occasion to speak later, but what Millet meant it to represent— the story he had to tell—he has himself put into words so perfectly that one must quote him again.

He says: "I have tried to show that she is neither a water-carrier nor yet a servant, but simply a woman drawing water for the use of her household—to make soup for her husband and children. I have tried to make her look as if she were carrying neither more nor less than the weight of the buckets full of water; and that through the kind of grimace which the load she bears forces her to make, and the blinking of her eyes in the sunlight, you should be able to see the air of rustic kindness on her face. I have avoided, as I always do, with a sort of horror, everything that might verge on the sentimental. On the contrary, I have tried to make her do her work simply and cheerfully, without regarding as a burden this act which, like other household duties, is part of her daily task, and the habit of her life. I have also tried to make people feel the freshness of the well, and to show by its ancient air how many generations have come there before her to draw water."

Now, if I had told you that this was what I read in the picture, you might imagine that I had read *into* it what Millet himself had never thought of putting there; but you have the artist's own word for it that this "literature" was intentional—was, in-

Plate 8.—"Death of St. Francis," by Giotto.

In the Church of Santa Croce, Florence.

deed, the main intention. You cannot
have that assurance often, and in the picture I am going to mention next you will
have to use your own judgment as to
whether or not I am right in my reading.
It is a picture owned by a collector in Chicago, an exquisite work by a true painter
who, at the time it was painted, came
nearer to the quality of the old Dutch masters than almost any other modern has
done—it is Alfred Stevens's *"Une Veuve"*
(Pl. 3). It is, I say, exquisitely painted,
and would be delightful to look at if it had
no story whatever; but what I want you
to observe, now, is the way the story is
told. It dates from the sixties of the last
century, and the costume and the accessories are of the period to which it belongs.
In an elegant interior, panelled in white
and gold, a pretty young widow in a vo-
luminous black gown leans back in the
depths of a red velvet divan, her hands
clasped in her lap with a gesture of ner-

vous indecision. On the slender-legged stand beside her are a little silver bell, to show that she is accustomed to being waited upon, a bound book, and a couple of paper-covered novels—just enough to indicate a refined and rather unoccupied existence. On the seat of the divan lies a great bouquet of flowers in its wrapping of white paper, and on the floor at her feet is the envelope, seal uppermost, of the note that has come with the flowers. The story is very unlike Millet's. Its mixture of sentiment and delicate irony is as different from Millet's simple earnestness as the rank of this fashionable lady is different from that of Millet's peasant woman. But the art of the telling is of the same kind—there is the same clarity, the same precision, the same reticence. "Persons and things are here for a purpose" and there is not one detail that is not necessary, not one "useless accessory."

There are a number of Stevens's early

pictures of much the same quality, and if any one is tempted to think their fine literary tact a matter of no moment, and entirely beside the bargain, he had better compare them with the same artist's later works, in which the love of elegance deteriorates into a love of bric-a-brac and the painter of genteel comedy becomes little better than a very skilful master of still-life.

I hope I have proved that much of our modern scorn for the story-telling picture is undeserved, and that there must be something worthy of serious attention in a side of art that has occupied the greatest masters since the practice of painting began. Yet there must be some cause for that scorn—there must be some reason why the mere epithet "story-telling," applied to a picture, has become a term of reproach. I think there are three main reasons for this state of affairs: painters have told stories that were too trivial; they have told stories that, however important and interesting in themselves, were ill-fitted for pictorial narration; and they have, partly because of this initial fault in the choice of the story to be told, told stories badly.

I have heard a little anecdote that illustrates pretty well one of these faults, as well as the modern suspicion of any interest in a picture other than the purely pictorial. A modern painter had painted a girl resting upon the sea-steps of a Venetian palace, and on the step below her he had painted a little crab at which she was looking. But his conscience troubled him on the score of that crab, and he gravely consulted a friend as to whether it ought not to be painted out, as introducing too much literary interest! Well, I laughed, at first, when I heard the tale, but afterward I found myself sympathizing with the artist and his scruples. I could not swallow that crab myself! And then it occurred to me that perhaps it was only the painter's reason that was wrong. The crab was not "too literary"; it was not literary enough. The interest it introduced was a slight and trivial one. As regards the girl it was a "useless accessory" and the story of the girl and her fatigue, or her idle dreams, would have been better told without it.

To be fitted for pictorial treatment a story should have some degree of importance and of universal interest, and it should be such a story as may be told in lines and colors, with no necessary reliance on the written word, or on anything outside its frame, for the explanation of its essential features. Then it must be told "fully and forcibly," without the frittering away of interest on the unimportant. Even the light stories of eighteenth-century French art have something of this necessary universality—they appeal to a permanent, if not a high, element in human nature. The stories of Michelangelo and of Millet are of the most fundamental and universal interest to mankind. The intelligibility of a story may be greatly aided by the degree in which it is well known to every one, and Rembrandt's Bible stories, like Michelangelo's myths of the Creation, are greatly helped by this universal knowledge, though his own genius for pictorial imagination was his main reliance. It is when we have, in art, stories that of themselves have little import, as with so many modern English pictures; stories that cannot be told by the means at the disposal of the painter, as often with Hogarth; stories that are poorly or falsely and melodramatically told, as with Greuze, that the story-telling picture justifies our contempt of it.

You have heard Millet describe Poussin's manner of painting a death-bed scene —now see Greuze's way of doing it in "The Punished Son" (Pl. 4). Look at the daughter at the left whose child tugs at her, note her gesture of despair and the careful disarrangement of her fichu— for, even in his most moral mood, Greuze must always give a little spice for the voluptuary. Look at the other daughter, beyond the bed, at her wild excitement and outstretched arm, as if she were dashing a scorpion from the brow of the dying man. Look at the attitudes of any of the figures, and try to imagine for a moment that you are a spectator of anything but a theatrical performance. This is not story-telling, or is story-telling only in the sense in which we were reproached with the habit in our infancy. It is telling lies. And the jugs and warming pans and crutches that clutter the floor are perfect examples of useless accessories.

So much for how not to tell a story: for an instance of the story that cannot be told clearly in art we shall go to Hogarth. He was a real painter, almost a great one, at his best, but he wanted to do more than painting can properly do. So, in his series of moral tales, he is forced to all sorts of expedients to make his meaning plain. We will take him at his best and most mature, in the admirably painted "Marriage A-la-Mode." The first scene represents "The Contract" (Pl. 5), and the artist wants to tell us all sorts of things. This is a loveless marriage, so the contracting couple are placed ostentatiously back to back, although there is nothing for the bridegroom to look at and he must smirk at empty space. The bride is, for the same reason, playing with her engagement ring on her handkerchief, instead of leaving it on her finger; and, as she is afterward to have an affair with the young lawyer, he is already flirting with her before both families. The new house which is building for the young couple is seen through the open window and, lest you should think it any other house, the parson is compar-

Plate 9.—"The Virgin in Glory," by Perugino.

In the Pinacoteca, Bologna.

ing it with the plainly lettered plan. The father of the bridegroom has an actual family tree to which he can point with one hand while he points to himself with the other, and the document which the bride's father offers him is conspicuously labelled "Mortgage." Even the contract must be carefully held sidewise, as no one would ever hold it, in order that the endorsement may be read. Well, the story is certainly told, but not by pictorial means. And Hogarth cannot escape from this shoring up and buttressing of his story by the written word. In the second scene of this same series we have the steward's packet with the paper on top marked "Bill" in large letters, and the book on the floor is opened at the title-page—which, by the way, is where a title-page never is—that we may read "Hoyle on Whist," and know what game was playing the night before. The only alternative to this sort of thing, if one insists on telling stories of this elaborate sort, is to paint a picture which may be fairly comprehensible after one has read the catalogue, but which means anything or nothing without its title.

It is the unfitness of many stories for telling in the language of painting that makes so many historical pictures altogether unsatisfactory and dismal. Let us suppose an American painter proposing to paint the Signing of the Emancipation Proclamation. Here is a subject of great dignity—of overwhelming importance— but how is its dignity and importance to be expressed? You will have a number of people gathered about a table, and one of them will be signing something, but unless you resort to a written label you have no means of telling what that something is. Even so, I have conceded too much. Some one is writing something, but it may be anything, from his signature on a State paper to a washing-list, so far as you can tell from the action itself. The best you can make of the subject is a portrait group, like Rembrandt's "Syndics of the Cloth Hall." As such it may be admirable, but it will not be the Signing of the Emancipation Proclamation except by courtesy, call it what you please.

Or take another historical subject that has actually been painted, "Washington Crossing the Delaware." Here there are more pictorial elements—the river with its floating ice is a good subject for a landscape painter, and the boats with their crews, in strong action, rowing or pushing off the ice cakes, afford fine opportunities for figure drawing. But can you tell what went before this crossing or is to come after it? Can you give any notion of the real and essential meaning of the incident? And how are you to make your hero conspicuous among the crowd of other actors? You can make him stand when others are seated; you can wrap him in a blowing cloak and give him an expression of brooding intentness; and you can relieve his well-known profile against the sky and put an American flag behind him. You will have made it plain that your subject is Washington crossing a river in the winter, and perhaps the historical knowledge of your audience may be expected to supply the rest—but you will have rendered your picture immortally absurd.

So great is this difficulty of the historical subject that I can recall only one instance in the whole history of art where it is entirely and satisfactorily overcome, Velazquez's "Surrender of Breda" (Pl. 6). The subject was, for once, admirably fitted to expression in graphic art, and the artist has, to use Millet's phrase again, "found an arrangement that gives full and striking expression to his idea." It is the surrender of a town that is taking place, and the character of the background makes it sufficiently plain that the scene is in the Low Countries—it is possible, indeed, that, to one who knows the region well enough, the localization is even more precise. The types and the costumes are sufficient evidence that it is a Dutch commander who is surrendering to a Spaniard, and we do not need to recognize the portraits of Justin of Nassau and Spinola to understand all that is necessary. To the right a great horse, a few heads, and twenty or thirty tall lances against the sky figure the Spanish army. To the left are the guards of the Dutch general with their shorter pikes and halberds. Justin bends low before his victor, who places a kindly hand upon his shoulder, and between their dark figures is a shield-shaped space of brilliant light in the midst of which, and almost in the exact middle of the picture, the key of the surrendered city stands out sharply. It is the key of the composition and of the story no less than of Breda.

If the story to be told could often be expressed as clearly and as fully as it is in this instance, we should hear less objection to historical painting as a manner of artistic production.

But it is just in the one situation where there is a natural public demand for the historical subject that that kind of subject, particularly in this country, is most difficult to handle successfully. In asking that our public buildings should be decorated with paintings relating to our own history our people are only asking what every other people has asked from time immemorial. Unfortunately our history is short, our modern costume formless and ugly, and American historical subjects particularly unfitted for pictorial and, especially, for decorative treatment. I have said that the highest walk of figure painting concerns itself with "the human figure, nude or so draped as to express rather than to conceal its structure and movement," but the costume of the last

three centuries lends itself little to such
treatment of the figure, and the painter
who cares greatly for the expressiveness
of the body will feel little attraction to belt
buckles and brass buttons. Again, mural
painting, from its association with architecture, is especially an art of formal and
symmetrical composition, of monumental
arrangements and balanced lines and
masses, and such composition necessarily
destroys all illusion of veracity in the de-
piction of an historical incident. Finally,
decoration demands sumptuous and brilliant, or, at any rate, studied and beautiful, color; and too many of our historical
subjects afford little opportunity for this.

Thus a love for the human figure, a love
for monumental and truly decorative
composition, and a love for color, all tend
to lead our mural painters away from the
historical subject and toward an allegorical, or rather symbolic, treatment, and
this tendency is strong almost in exact pro-

[71]

portion as the artist affected by it is a real decorator by temperament and training. Nor is the tendency a new one; it has existed since there was an art of painting. The walls of Italy are covered with frescos and the palace of the Doges is lined with paintings, nearly all of which were intended to have some historical implication, but there are, apart from the renderings of sacred narrative, relatively few strictly historical pictures among them, and these are seldom the most effective. The most triumphantly decorative are allegories, naïf in the Spanish Chapel or the ceilings of Pinturicchio, superb in Veronese's "Venice Enthroned."

It is true that the strictly historical subject may, on occasion, be so treated as to reduce its essentially undecorative character to a minimum. You may simplify it in arrangement and, in some cases, arrive almost at a monumental composition; you may eliminate light and shade and

Plate 10.—"The Last Supper," by Leonardo da Vinci.

In Milan.

avoid strong contrasts and projecting modelling; you may weaken its pictorial character until it consents to stay on the wall, and to do little harm to the architectural ensemble, if it does no good to it. But when all is done it will not be essential decoration. You will still have to choose between historical pictures which are, at best, imperfectly and negatively decorative, and have lost much of their force in becoming so, and true monumental decorations, perfectly suited to their place and function, but symbolical rather than real in their treatment of history.

If you believe—and I cannot see how you can help believing it—that the first end of a decoration is to decorate, there can be no doubt which you will prefer.

The choice, once made, will carry with it much more than an increase of decorative beauty—it will greatly enlarge the scope of the ideas you may express, and increase the clarity and force with which you may express them. I chose, a while ago, to illustrate the difficulty of the purely historical subject, the theme of the Signing of the Emancipation Proclamation, and pointed out how it reduced itself, if realistically treated, to a man writing at a table, in the presence of a number of other men. But admit the element of symbolism and the difficulty vanishes at once. You may paint "Lincoln Emancipating the Slave," in a way that shall be perfectly intelligible to every one, and you may go further and convey the whole meaning of the struggle for freedom and suggest the vast upheaval of the Civil War by a use of allegorical figures. Velazquez was particularly happy, in his "Surrender of Breda," in finding a subject suited to realistic expression and in finding, also, the exact expression needed. But even that prince of naturalists, when he would paint "the Expulsion of the Moors," had to fall back on allegory like all the world before him.

From the point of view of expression as from the point of view of form there is really no alternative. We must admit the symbolical or we must give up monumental and decorative painting altogether.

To what degree the symbolical element shall displace entirely the historical must be a question, largely, of the temper and ability of the artist. Some will feel most at home in an atmosphere of pure symbolism, where nothing shall hamper their sense of beauty or intrude considerations of fact or costume. Others will be able to include a good deal of fact and costume without feeling that it impedes their creation of decorative beauty. In this style of partly historical, partly symbolic, art are two notably successful works by American artists, one in sculpture and one in painting, Saint-Gaudens's "Sherman" and Blashfield's decoration in the Baltimore Court House, "Washington Laying Down his Commission" (Pl. 7). In the "Sherman" the contrast between the modern soldier and the antique victory troubles some people who would have felt no incongruity, probably, if the general had been a warrior in fifteenth-century armor, or had worn the habit of a Roman Emperor, though in either case the mingling of fact and fiction would have been the same. So swiftly is time foreshortened as it recedes into the past that Washington, in blue and buff, seems naturally enough placed amid the half-mediæval, half-ancient, costumes of the symbolical figures about him. They are all removed from the present, which is, for us, the only real, and seem equally to belong to an ideal world. The effect of the whole is sumptuously decorative, while the larger implications of the story to be told are much more clearly expressed than they could be by a realistic representation of the scene that occurred at Annapolis in 1783.

III

DESIGN

PERHAPS the greatest weakness of modern art is the relative neglect of what is ordinarily called composition, or what I prefer to call by the good old word design. The word composition means, of course, the putting together of the picture, and seems to imply a more or less mechanical assemblage of separately existing parts. The word design conveys the finer and truer idea of an original guiding thought, a principle of unity, out of which the parts and details of a picture are developed by a natural and organic growth. You compose a pudding or a black draught—you design a work of art. Yet the word composition is a convenient one, and one so commonly understood that I shall use it interchangeably with the word design.

Whatever it is to be called, that the thing itself is rather out of fashion there can be no doubt. Our tendency has been to exalt the other parts of the art of painting at the expense of this fundamental one of design, and to decry and belittle composition as a thing of small or no importance. Indeed, if one may believe all one hears, its very existence has been denied; for a well-known and justly admired American painter has been quoted as telling his pupils that "There is no such thing as composition." If he ever said so, one is left in doubt as to just what he can have meant. It is possible that he intended to say that there is no science of composition, and no valid rules for it—that design is, and must be, a matter of instinct and of unconscious creative action on the part of the artist. In that case, what is true in his statement is equally true of drawing

and color and handling. In all these
things the business of the artist is to create,
and to leave to others the task of finding
out the reasons for the form of his creations. It is possible, in any art, to formu-
late principles to account for what has
first been done—it is impossible, by the
application of rules based on these principles, to create a new and vital work.
This is not a reason for neglecting the
study of the masterpieces of art, for
ignorance was never yet creative. It is
simply the statement, in another form,
that the artist, however well trained, must
be an artist born, and work as the artist
has always worked.

It is possible, also, that what was meant
to be expressed was merely a personal
preference for informal and expressive
design over formal and monumental design; for the composition of the isolated
easel picture over the composition of the
great mural painting. If so, it was the ex-

pression of a preference so common in our time as to be nearly universal; a preference which has caused us to place on the walls of great public buildings pictures that seem to defy rather than to enrich the design of the surrounding architecture; a preference which has led to the writing of text-books on composition that include in the list of their don'ts nearly all the things which a study of the great masters would inculcate as things to do.

Whatever else was meant, it is almost inconceivable that a literal denial of the existence of composition, or design, can have been intended, for that would have been the denial to the arts of the one thing they have in common, of the one great fundamental and unifying principle that makes art art. Design is arrangement, is order, is selection. Design is the thing that makes a work of art a unit, that makes it a whole rather than a hap-hazard collection of unrelated things or a slice of un-

Plate 11.—" La Disputà," by Raphael.

In the Vatican, Rome.

assimilated nature. It does not merely concern itself with great decorative compositions or arrangements of many figures —it is necessarily present in the simplest problems art can set itself. Suppose you are to paint a portrait head. There will be questions of drawing, of character and expression, of light and shade and color, of the handling of your material, to all of which you must find answers; but before you can consider any of these things, there will be the initial question: where are you to place the head on your canvas? How far from the top and the bottom, how far from the left or right hand border? And what is the shape of your canvas to be, rectangular or circular or oval, and what shall be the proportion of height to width? This is the fundamental problem of design, the problem of the division of space. If you are going to do a little more of the figure, other problems will come into play. Shall you include the hands, and, if so, where shall you place them? That is the problem of the balancing of dominant and subordinate masses. What is the general silhouette of your figure, and where shall it cut the borders of your canvas? That is the problem of line. If you do not settle it intentionally and well it will settle itself accidentally and, in all probability, badly. The problems of design are essentially the same in everything you do; they only become more complicated as the subject becomes more complex.

If you are to paint a still-life it is evident that you must arrange the objects somehow—they will not come together of themselves. You might, conceivably, begin a portrait and wait for a happy accident—a spontaneous pose of the sitter—to give you the arrangement of the hands: you cannot wait for the copper kettle and the dead fish to place themselves agreeably. And still less can nature or accident determine your composition of a number of figures, unless you rely entirely upon snap shots. If you have any intention, any story to tell, any idea to express—if it is no more than the idea of a crowd—you *must* arrange your figures, well or ill. Even in landscape painting of the most naturalistic kind, where it is not uncommon to-day to accept what nature gives, abdicating the right to put in or leave out and retaining only that right of choosing an agreeable view which the photographer exercises equally with the painter—even there, though you may reproduce a natural landscape as literally as you are able, you must determine where to cut it off. You must decide where to make the division between your chosen matter and the rest of nature which you reject, you must think whether your material will go best onto an upright canvas or an oblong one, and what are to be its proportions and dimensions. In that act you are exercising the art of design. You cannot escape from design; you cannot avoid composing. You may compose badly but compose you must.

And if the demands of design are fundamental they are also universal. It is not only your lines and masses that must be composed, but your light and shade, your color, your very brushmarks must be arranged; and the task of composition is not done until the last touch has been placed upon the canvas, although, for the sake of convenience, the term composition, or design, is generally limited to the arrangement of lines and masses, the arrangement of the other elements of the picture being considered separately.

As design is the underlying and unifying principle of every work of art, so it is the classic principle, par excellence, the principle which makes for order and stability and clarity and all that the classic spirit holds most dear. It is conservative in its nature, and tends to preserve the old

molds even when new matter is put into
them. It holds on to tradition and keeps
up the connection with the past. It
changes, but it changes more slowly than
almost any other element of art. Great
and original power of design is more rare
than any other of the powers of an artist
and a radically new form of design is very
nearly inconceivable. Artists will make
a thousand new observations of nature
and almost entirely alter the contents of a
work of art before they make any but
slight changes in the pattern in which it is
cast; and in all the history of painting the
men are but a handful who have made any
material addition to the resources of the
designer. If in our own day we seem to
have cut loose from tradition and to have
lost our connection with the great design
of the past it is not because we have suddenly acquired a surprising degree of designing power and are inventing a new
and modern art of composition, but be-

cause most of us have forgotten altogether how to compose and are trying to get on without any design at all; the result being bad design and mere chaos. Wherever, in modern art as in the art of the past, you find an artist of real power of design—and we have had such—you find the note of classicism, of respect for tradition, of connection with everything fine and noble that has gone before.

This conservatism of design follows naturally from the fact that it is not imitative of nature, and is therefore unaffected by the investigation of natural appearances. It is, of course, founded on natural laws—on the laws of sight and on the laws of the human mind—but it is only accidentally and occasionally that it is directly influenced by anything outside itself. The naturalistic temper will, as it has done at various times, lead to the neglect of composition: it will not lead to new discoveries in composition. The study of anatomy revolutionized and greatly enriched the drawing of the human figure; the study of natural light and color has added something to the resources of the painter, if it has also subtracted something from them; the only study that has ever greatly helped the designer is the study of design as it has been practised before him. To look long at the great compositions of the master designers of the world; to try to find in them, not hard and fast rules of what to do and what to avoid, but the guiding principles on which they are built; to steep one's self in tradition; and then to set one's self to invent new forms which shall be guided by the principles and contained within the boundaries of the old—that is the only way to study design. It is precisely because design must be studied in this way, because it makes for tradition and continuity and leads away from a too exclusive study of nature, that, from the classic point of view, for which I speak, the study of design is the most salutary discipline possible in this too naturalistic age. If I could have my way in the training of young artists I should insist upon their spending a good deal of time in the study and designing of pure ornament, not that they might learn the "historic styles"—though that, too, would have its advantages—but that they might learn how independent fine design is of its content and how slight may be the connection between art and nature.

In all design concerned with the beautifying of surfaces, as painting is, from the simplest treatment of ornament to the most complicated of naturalistic pictures, the ends to be sought and the means of attaining these ends are the same. First, there is the division of the whole space to be treated into a number of smaller spaces, or masses, which shall be agreeable in their relation to each other and of interesting and beautiful shapes. Some of these

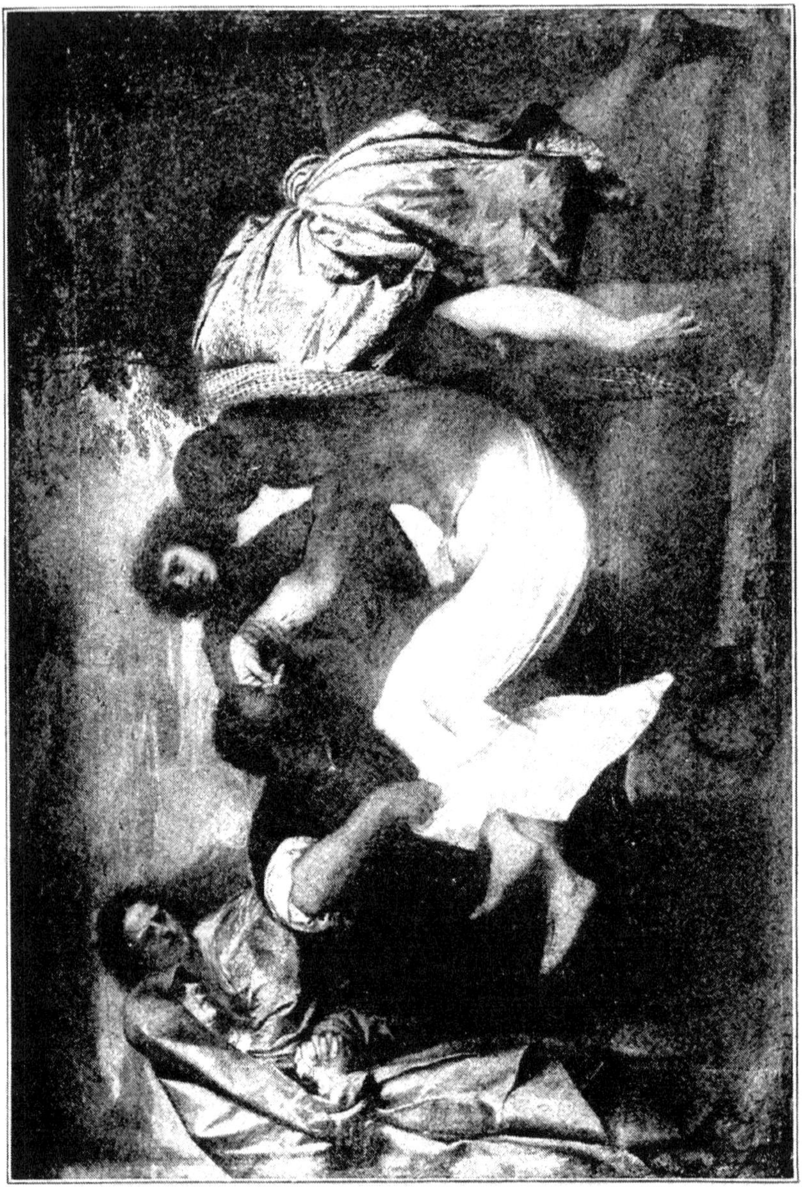

spaces will be filled with minor divisions and enriched with details, while others will be left comparatively simple, like the background of ornament, and we have thus that balance of filled and empty spaces which is one of the great beauties of fine design. Some one of the masses will, by size, by position, or by isolation, sometimes by all three means, be made more important than the others, and this principle of subordination will be carried throughout the design, each mass which is subordinate to the principal one having other attendant masses subordinated to it.

After the division of space comes the unification by line. The whole composition will be bound together by a series of lines, either the edges of the masses or interior lines within them, and these lines will not only be agreeable in themselves but will be so arranged as to lead the eye easily and without jar or fatigue, from one mass to another, bringing it finally to rest on the dominant mass of the composition. And these lines will have characters of their own, entirely apart from anything they may represent. Horizontal lines will suggest repose, vertical lines will suggest rigidity and stability, curved lines will convey the idea of motion; and the curves will differ among themselves, some being soft and voluptuous, others resilient and tonic.

In the use of these primary elements of composition a number of subsidiary principles will come into play: The principle of balance, either of like subordinate masses either side a central dominant, which is symmetrical and monumental composition, or of unlike masses at different distances from an ideal centre, which is free or pictorial composition, though the Japanese use it in ornament: the principle of repetition, the extreme form of which is the continuous frieze or border, but which is constantly used in pictures: the principle of contrast, the straight line making the curve seem more graceful, the curve making the straight line seem more uncompromising and more rigid.

The structure of the design being thus formed it will be enriched and re-enforced by the use of light and dark and by the use of color. In a simple panel of ornament, for instance, the filled spaces, that is the ornament itself, will be either darker or lighter than the ground or empty spaces; or they will be of a different color from the empty spaces, without any greatly marked difference of value. Or the filled spaces may be both lighter and darker than the ground, as they would be in sculpture in relief. The dominance of the most important mass may be increased by making it the lightest or the darkest or the most powerfully colored mass, or by giving it the sharpest contrast of light and dark; and however this is done certain of the subsidiary masses will be given a secondary importance by a less marked use of the same means.

So far the process is identical, whether the content of the design is pure ornament or a great figure painting, but as we approach the free design of the easel picture a new element comes into play. Ornamental design is design in two dimensions only, and decorative painting always tends to retain, or to return to, two dimensional composition. But in proportion as painting becomes desirous and able to convey the illusion of space it begins to compose in the third dimension also. The things it represents have not only an elevation but a ground plan, and the ground plan must be as thoroughly designed as the elevation. The distances of one mass from another in the direction of the depth of the picture must be as carefully proportioned as the vertical and lateral distances, and the lines traced upon the ideal ground plan must be as beautiful as those visible upon the vertical surface.

These are, as well as I can explain them in brief compass, the immutable principles of design: few in number, but admitting of so much variety in their application that all the great compositions that have ever been made have not begun to exhaust the possible combinations—there is room for an infinite number of fine compositions, still. The extent to which these principles govern the work of the great designers is almost incredible until one has convinced one's self of it by prolonged study. Their scope is co-extensive with the work, and in the masterpieces of design there is absolutely no room for accident. Every smallest detail, each fold of drapery, each leaf in each smallest spray of leafage, is where it must be, and is of its proper form and inevitable size to play its part in the symphony of design.

It could no more be somewhere else or of some other shape than a note could be of another pitch in a musical composition. Any change in it would change the character of the whole. Designs of this perfection are rare, of course, but they exist; and in some of the compositions of Raphael and Veronese you could not change so much as a tendril of hair or a ring on a finger without loss.

The design of early and primitive artists is, naturally enough, extremely simple and formal. From Giotto to Raphael there is only a very gradual enrichment of a manner of composition which remains essentially the same. The pictures of this time are almost exclusively of two types: the narrative composition, devoted to the telling of Gospel stories or to the lives of the Saints; and the devotional composition or altar-piece.

The narrative composition, in early work, tends to the condition of the frieze or bas-relief. The figures are apt to be in profile and are nearly always in one plane, and they are rather isolated without much connection into groups. With all its simplicity this form of design is capable of great expressiveness, and, from its very limitations, is admirably fitted for architectural decoration. It was perhaps, involuntarily that the work of Giotto was so unfailingly decorative, for the simplicity of division and the composition on one plane were inevitable at the stage of development which the art of painting had then reached. But the dignity and the inventiveness, within the limits of what was then possible, are the master's own. There have been more complete painters than Giotto, because there have been great men who came at periods of fuller ripeness in their art; but there have been few artists of greater essential power as designers. Again and again he found the best arrangement for the telling of his story, and settled the lines on which his successors were willing to work for a century or two. Such a composition as his "Death of St. Francis" (Pl. 8) remains to this day as simple and noble in its great lines and masses as anything that has been done and it would be hard to better it except in detail, or even to better its details without losing something of its majesty.

The devotional picture, the purpose of which was not to tell a story but merely to present objects for worship, descends from the Byzantine ancona, and was, at first, made up of a number of separate panels, framed together into a great altar-piece. There would be a Madonna and Child in the middle panel, probably on a larger scale than the other figures, and rows of saints on either side, each in its own niche. The first step in advance amounted to little more than removing the interior divisions, leaving the figures much as they

Plate 13.—"Pallas Driving away Mars," by Tintoretto.
In the Ducal Palace, Venice.

were, even to the greater size of the central figure. Except for the elimination of this discrepancy in size there was little further development of this form of composition until Raphael took hold of it, but its essentially architectural character was appreciated, and it was applied to other than religious subjects. It became, especially, and has remained to this day, the natural form of composition for the lunette, or semicircular space, with its greatest height in the middle, where the central figure would come. But, in altar-pieces or decorative allegories, you may yet see, in the work of Perugino (Pl. 9), how the subsidiary figures stand in a row, each almost as much alone as if it still had its own frame around it. Meantime the narrative composition had become richer and more complex, and the two forms met in Leonardo's "Last Supper" (Pl. 10), half narrative, half devotional, where the apostles, instead of sitting more or less equidistant from each other, are played about into groups of three and bound together with interlacing lines of arms and draperies. It is the first complete and fully perfected instance of formal design in modern art.

Then came Raphael, the greatest master of formal design that the world has seen, and gave us the still unequalled models of decorative composition. His fecundity and variety are astonishing. In one room, the Stanza della Segnatura in the Vatican, he has given us the perfect examples of composition for the circular medallion, the rectangular panel, the semicircular lunette, the segmental lunette, and the pierced lunette, or lunette with an opening cut through it; and in the second of these chambers of the Vatican are two other pierced lunettes, entirely different and equally admirable, the "Mass of Bolsena" and the "Deliverance of Peter." Besides these he has shown us, in Santa Maria

della Pace, how to design a frieze inter-
rupted by a central arch and, in the
Farnesina, how to design a series of tri-
angular pendentives; while a multitude
of Madonnas and other pictures of smaller
size are, almost invariably, masterpieces
of composition. Yet he has introduced few
absolute novelties, the chief of these being
a strictly limited use of the third dimension. He still composes laterally instead of
composing in depth, but, in the "Dis-
puta" (Pl. 11), he has for the first time
thrown the centre of his composition back
and advanced the sides, achieving an effect
as if the lunette had become a great semi-
dome or apse. It is as architectural as
composition in the flat, but while it definitely limits it also enlarges the apparent
space and gives one breathing-room and
a consequent sense of ease and enhanced
well-being. Further than this it is dangerous for purely decorative design to go,
and composition in depth rarely has gone

much further in the hands of true deco-
rators.

This whole composition, the earliest
and the most formal of Raphael's great
frescoes in the Vatican, is perhaps the
most perfect of any for its decorative and
symbolic purpose, and it is worth a little
study to see how he has designed it much
in the same way that a designer of ornament might fill the same space. The most
important object in the picture, from the
point of view of the story he had to tell,
is the Host upon the altar, for the real
presence in the celebration of the Mass is
the central doctrine of Catholic theology.
It is a small object and cannot be given
predominance by size—it must attain it
by position and by isolation. He places its
little circle in the midst of a broad band
of empty space, the only one, which ex-
tends from one end of the design to the
other, and just at the level of the spring
of the arch, so that the whole composition

radiates from it as from a centre. Below
it is the church on earth, above it the
heavenly host—it dominates earth and
heaven. Immediately above is the figure
of Christ, in a great circular glory, with
the Virgin and John Baptist on His right
and left hands and the first and third Persons of the Trinity above and below Him
—a compact group of great size and importance, yet a less important centre than
the Host because less isolated. From this
group sweeps to right and left the great
semicircle of Apostles and Prophets,
seated upon the level clouds, and this
semicircle is repeated, higher up, by that
of the Angels. Below are Popes, Bishops,
Cardinals, poets, Fathers of the Church,
disposed in two great, wedge-shaped
masses, narrowing toward the central rectangle of the altar; and the presence of a
door at one end of the wall has led to the
introduction of balustrades at either cor-
ner which happily echo this rectangle,

making it the apex of a triangle in the ground plan, while the long, horizontal lines of the steps and pavement give stability and repose to the whole design.

So far, it is all formality and geometrical planning; but now the element of variety enters. It is very slight in the upper portion of the composition, only the leaning sidewise of St. Stephen breaking the uniformity of the rank of Saints; but it is almost infinite below—figures standing, sitting, kneeling, leaning, gathering into clumps and scattering again, their heads forming an intricate and ingenious skyline, yet always controlled by some hidden principle of unity, line balancing line and mass answering to mass by subtle and hardly discoverable conformities. Each group—each single figure almost—is as wonderful in its design as the great whole of which it forms a part. I could point out some of these minor felicities of arrangement, but it would take too long, and the student will get more out of the effort to find them for himself. And, long as I have studied the picture, I by no means understand it all, nor do I hope ever to do so. I only know that it is supremely right and perfect, altogether and forever satisfying.

I shall not attempt to analyze any other composition in such detail as this. My object is to show what design is, in one great example, and to set you to looking for it in other works of art. And you will find it in places where at first you would not think of looking for it. The splendor of Venetian color and the richness of Venetian light and shade have so blinded us to the presence of anything else in the works of Titian and Tintoretto that it is only after special study that one realizes their power of design. But if you will look over any of the old-fashioned histories of art which are illustrated with cuts in little more than outline, and bad outline at that, you will find that, after color and light and

shade have been eliminated, and drawing
denatured, there remains an indestructible
element in the work of these men which an-
nounces, at the first glance, the presence of
a master. That element is, and can be,
nothing but design. It is more usually the
free design suited to easel-painting—a form
of art practically invented by Giorgione—
but is none the less masterly and complete
on that account. Take, for example,
Titian's "Entombment" (Pl. 12) and see
how the lines of the figures encompass the
dead Christ; how every arm and hand and
fold of drapery is played into a series of
curves that sympathize with and accent-
uate the helpless droop of that dead body;
how absolute and inevitable is the spacing
within the frame; how impossible it would
be to alter the smallest detail without destroying the harmony of the whole. Or
take Tintoretto at his best, in the wonderful "Pallas Driving away Mars" (Pl. 13)
and see how everything in the picture re-

inforces and lends added strength to the push of the goddess's arm. And for an exquisite bit of contrast, see how the stiff straightness of Pallas's lance relieves and yet enhances the luxuriance of the curves, noting, at the same time, how the different angles of the two lances, as if sprung from a common centre like the spokes of a wheel, set everything swinging over to the right and send Mars tottering out of the picture faster, even, than his own attitude would carry him. This is design, and design of the best. As for Veronese, who added to all the other Venetian qualities a gayety of feeling and a brilliancy of workmanship which tend still more to disguise the underlying structure, he is, whether for formal and monumental or for free and fantastic composition, second only to Raphael, if he is second to any one. He is a decorator born, and the decorator, whatever his other gifts, is always preeminently and fundamentally a designer.

Since the time of these great sixteenth century masters there has been no new discovery in design. Its principles have been differently applied and have been applied to various purposes, but there has been no addition to the resources of the designer. Rubens, with all his giant-like strength and almost appalling abundance and fecundity, was by essential temper a classicist and a lover of tradition; only his was a classicism modified by and appropriate to his age, an age of the Baroque in architecture and of luxuriousness in life. In every part of his art he founded his practice upon that of his predecessors, and his composition is the composition of the great Venetians rendered a little looser, a little more florid. The straight line is almost entirely banished, the curved lines are more redundant and less severe, and have a strong tendency to the double, or S-shaped, curve, while the whole pattern is more irregular and picturesque. None the less is it a pattern, complete and self-contained, as inevitable in the logical connection of the parts with the main idea of the whole as one of Raphael's. Such grasp of composition as forces every limb of every one of the myriad figures in the small "Last Judgment" into its predestined place in the huge, if sprawling design—for the design is huge though the canvas is small—is almost disconcerting.

During the same years in which Rubens was producing his Baroque classicism a classicist of a very different sort was at work in Rome. For Poussin, a man of cold temper and powerful intellect, the colorists did not exist. He founded his style on Raphael and, above all, on the study of the antique, and his composition is severe almost to baldness, but grandly expressive. Being more in harmony with his age, Rubens was immensely the more influential of the two. His composition, with slight modifications, becomes the composition of the whole of the seventeenth and eighteenth centuries, while in such splendid pieces of bravura as the "Rape of the Daughters of Leucippus" (Pl. 14) or the Medici series in The Louvre, we have the model of almost everything that Delacroix produced. Rubens is the fountainhead of modern art—Poussin has had few disciples. The greatest of these is Jean François Millet, whose description of his favorite master's "Testament of Eudamitas" you have already heard.

Of Millet's own design, as austere as Poussin's and as expressive, no better example could be given than "The Gleaners" (Pl. 15). It is design reduced to the barely necessary, purged of all luxury or superfluity, the naked expression of one idea and no more. The field is divided into two broad bands by the horizon line, at about two-thirds of the height of the canvas, and the long sky line is broken only at the left by the simple mass of the wagon and the straw-stacks. Wholly within the lower division are the three figures, two of them forming a compact group, the third a little apart yet so near that a single sweeping curve would unite the three. The two are bent double to reach the ground, and their lines repeat each other almost exactly. The third is standing, but so stooped that the line of her body recalls and sympathizes with the stronger lines of the other two. That is all; but these few elements are placed with such perfect sense of weight and balance, the relations of the large and simple spaces to each other and to the enclosing border are so admirably right; the bounding and connecting lines are so noble and so expressive that nothing more could be asked for. Different as he was from Millet in every fibre of his artistic nature, it is by much such simple divisions of space and such economy of line that Whistler produces his finest effects. The design of both men is at the antipodes of the overflowing abundance and richness of that of Rubens; yet the severe and the luxurious are equally legitimate forms of design. Which one will prefer is a matter of temperament and of occasion—of what one has to do and of what one likes doing.

The great masters of design in portraiture, among the old masters, are Raphael, who was as wonderful as a portrait painter as he was as a decorator, and Holbein. Holbein also, as we know from a few paintings and many woodcuts, was a great figure designer, but, in his strongest years, he was permitted to produce little but portraits. These portraits, even the slightest drawings, are unfailingly perfect in design. The head is always in just the right spot on the canvas, the hands are at just the right distance from the head, the division of space between the figure and the background is always agreeable, the bounding line of the figure is always beautiful and always cuts the edge of the picture in the right place and at the right angle. Some of them are much more elaborate than others; but take one of the simplest of them, the incomparable "Erasmus" (Pl. 16) of the Louvre, and you will find it as admirable and perfect as a design as it is as a rendering of character—I do not know how to praise it more highly than that.

But the first half of the nineteenth century saw a master of design as great as any that ever lived, and I do not know but that some of the portraits of Ingres are the most complete and perfect examples of design as applied to portraiture in the whole range of art. For a design appropriate to and almost miraculously expressive of character and bodily habit it would be difficult to find anything approaching the "M. Bertin"; while for a design beautiful in its own right, rich, elaborate, gracious, yet with a lofty and serene austerity in its pure beauty, I know not where to find a parallel for the exquisite portrait of Mme. Rivière (Pl. 17) short of those Greek gems of which its oval form, no less than its artistic quality, reminds us.

I spoke, awhile ago, of design as preeminently the conservative and classic element in art. In no branch of art is this more true than in the painting of landscape. Landscape painting is a comparatively modern form of art, and modern discoveries concerning light and atmosphere have so transformed our view of nature that, were it not for this element of design, which has no naturalistic origin, modern landscape painting would have been in danger of losing all touch with the past and thereby losing, also, that power of evoking memories of former pleasures which is one of the great pleasure-giving resources of all art. Fortunately the first

Plate 14.—"The Daughters of Leucippus," by Rubens.

In the old Pinakothek at Munich.

great innovators in modern landscape were lovers of the past, and master designers. The detailed study of natural forms, the mystery of atmospheric effect, the glow of color or the delicate rendering of gradations of light were, with Rousseau and Corot, but the clothing of a pattern which was traditional and classic. It is this persistence of pattern which gives their work its air of permanence and finality—which makes it a part of the art of the world and of all time. With Corot (Pl. 18), especially, the classic feeling was so strong that his pictures give you echoes of everything noble and lovely that has been done, of Titian and Giorgione, fathers of landscape painting, no less than of the severe grandeur of Poussin and the clear grace of Claude.

And it is this conservative, and preservative, element of design that will save such of the work of the successors of Corot and Rousseau as the world shall permanently enjoy. Monet and his friends have undoubtedly made some discoveries about natural light and the means of representing it in painting—discoveries not so new perhaps, or so important as they thought them, but still discoveries—and in so far as they have done this, they have been of use to those that shall come after them, as the naturalists of the fifteenth century, with their studies of anatomy and perspective, were serviceable to their successors; but in so far as they have neglected design they have forgotten to be artists and contented themselves with being investigators. For without design there may be representation, but there can be no art.

This tendency to a comparative neglect of design, to allowing representation to become an end instead of a means, to making what should be an embroidery of light and color take the place of the structure that should underlie the embroidery—a tendency which is the common temptation of the modern painter— is particularly insidious and dangerous to the painter of landscape. He finds the rendering of natural effect so difficult and so absorbing that he can think of nothing else, and nature is so beautiful that she usurps, for him, the place of art. He is apt to be, in the first place, one to whom light and color mean more than line and mass, or he would have chosen figure painting as his vocation, and he has not the figure painter's dominating necessity to compose somehow, well or ill. As most of his work, nowadays, is done in the open air, he must paint rapidly while the effect lasts, and has no time for ponderation and delicate balancing of mass against mass and line against line. He habituates himself to taking snap-shots at things as they fly, satisfied if he can capture any reflection of the beauty of the scene before him, and contents himself with so much thought of composition as goes to the determination of what fragment of nature he may include within his frame.

The more to be admired are those painters whose native sense of design is so powerful as to give distinction and a classic grace even to their sketches from nature. One such, who has almost ceased to paint without ceasing to be an artist, is Charles A. Platt. First an etcher, then a painter of distinction, a member of the Society of American Artists, and now of the National Academy of Design, and a winner of the Webb Prize, he has produced a series of landscapes which, for elegance of line, dignity of spacing and beauty of arrangement are unique in our art. Some day, his pictures will be appreciated at their worth. Meanwhile, he has had to turn to another form of art and, as was the case with the great artists of the Renaissance, the same mastery of design that was so notable in his painting, has given him an assured place in the kindred art of Architecture.

Such refined design as Mr. Platt's has always been rare, but our art is not without other examples of the compatibility with the modern point of view of a real faculty for design. Even among the most forthright and least reflective of our painters—among those who seem to have placed truth far above beauty and with whom a certain almost violent effectiveness has taken the place of all subtler qualities—even in this muscular school of landscape there are different degrees of designing power; and it is, more than anything else, the possession of this power— the ability to give to each picture, no matter how instantaneously seen or swiftly rendered, the consistency of a pattern— that places such men as Gardner Symons and George Bellows above their companions.

But the strongest instance of such compatibility is the work of the great painter we have lately lost, Winslow Homer (Pl. 19). A modern of the moderns, so original that his art seems, at first sight, to have no connection with any other, such an independent observer that he has painted whole series of things seen by no one else, he was yet essentially a designer, and it is his design that gives his work its authority. He was hardly a draughtsman, at least so far as the drawing of the human figure is concerned; he was rarely a colorist, in the full sense, and was often content with little more than black and white; he was still less an accomplished craftsman. What he had was an extraordinary vigor and originality of observation, which provided the substance of his works, and an equally original and vigorous design which gave them their form. Almost every work of his contains a new and striking pattern to which every detail is subordinated—a

Plate 15.—"The Gleaners," by Millet.

In the Louvre.

pattern as new and as striking as the material it moulds, and admirably suited to the expression of that material. It is his powerful design, even more than his clearness of vision, that makes him the great artist he was—the greatest we have had in America and one of the greatest of the latter part of the nineteenth century in any country.

IV

DRAWING

THE conception and treatment of the subject make up the purely intellectual part of painting: design is the purely artistic or musical part of the art. With the present subject we reach the consideration of those elements of painting which are partly representative or imitative of nature, and which, on that account, have been most affected by the modern, naturalistic temper. That temper, which has led to indifference as to subject and neglect of design, has profoundly modified our conception of the representative elements of art; and this modification has, perhaps, been greatest as regards drawing. We still retain some idea of color as a means of artistic expression, and . still think of a colorist as something more than one who imitates with exactness the colors of nature: we have come to think of drawing as a mere matter of accurate observation, and of the draughtsman as one with a trained eye and hand who can "take a measure or follow a line." To get things of the right sizes and shapes—our notion of drawing has reduced itself nearly to that; and so we have become contemptuous of draughtsmanship as a thing necessary, indeed, in some degree, but not particularly meritorious. Finding that even this kind of drawing takes long training to acquire, we have supposed that it requires nothing else, and have considered it a thing, like spelling, to be learned by any diligent person, rating the ability to draw as low in reckoning the achievement of a painter as we should the ability to spell in summing up the work of a poet.

If it were true that "any one can learn to draw," this would be an odd excuse for those who have manifestly failed to do so: but it is not true, even of the limited kind of drawing we are considering. Any one who has ever had any connection with a school of art must know that it is only a very small proportion of the students who ever attain to any tolerable proficiency in drawing—who ever learn to get an approximation to the right sizes and shapes of things. To get these sizes and shapes with anything like real accuracy and delicacy requires so rare an organization that the possession of that alone is almost a passport to immortality. There is more to Holbein and Terborch, Metsu and Vermeer than their impeccable and, apparently, colorless draughtsmanship— their drawing is not so unaccented, so untinged by personality, so purely naturalistic as it looks—but even their accuracy is inimitable and their refinement the despair of any one who would attempt to imitate them. Their drawing is by no means merely photographic, though it often seems more accurate than the photograph itself, but even photographic drawing is so difficult that the world is full of painters to-day who have given up working against the camera and are trying to work with it—who have found that they cannot draw like a photograph and are letting photography do their drawing for them.

If there were no more to drawing than accuracy of imitation—than that "placing" of things which we too often accept for it—such a method might answer. But drawing is a great expressional art and deals with beauty and significance, not with mere fact. Its great masters are the greatest artists that ever lived, and high attainment in it has always been rarer than high attainment in color. Its tools are the line and so much of light and shade as is necessary to convey the sense of bulk and modelling, anything more being something added for its own beauty and expressiveness, not a part of the resources of the draughtsman. Its aims are, first, to develop in the highest degree the abstract beauty and significance possessed by lines in themselves, more or less independently of representation; second, to express with the utmost clearness and force the material significance of objects and, especially, of the human body. According as one or the other of these aims predominates we have one or the other of the two great schools into which draughtsmen may be divided. These schools may be typified by the greatest masters of each, the school of Botticelli, or the school of pure line; the school of Michelangelo, or the school of significant form. Between these lie all the law and the prophets. Of course no artist ever belonged entirely and exclusively to either school. It is always a matter of balance and the predominance of interest. Even a Botticelli tried to put some significant form inside

Plate 16.—"Erasmus," by Holbein.

In the Louvre.

his beautiful lines, and even Michelangelo gave thought to the abstract beauty of his lines apart from the significant form they bounded. To some extent apart from either school is the most difficult drawing of all to understand or to describe, the drawing of Rembrandt.

We are all so much, and so inevitably, bound by the conventions of our own time that to many an art student of to-day it will seem little less than absurd to call Botticelli a draughtsman at all. He could not foreshorten a leg or an arm, but drew them always at full length, exercising great ingenuity, at times, in so arranging his groups as to permit of this full length treatment. His use of light and shade is very restricted and he never gives the illusion of solidity and detachment from the background. His figures are attenuated, never very certain in their structure and articulation, and often faulty in proportion. The modern student, from the height of nearly five centuries of further study, looks down with amused superiority, conscious that all those things which were impossible for Botticelli are commonplace now, and within the power of every one. And yet the student is no more than a student whose work is not worth the paper it is drawn on—the master remains the master, as unique and unapproachable to-day as in his own time. The student can place things better—unless he is a rare genius, he will never draw one thousandth part so well.

A group which shows Botticelli at his best, yet with all or nearly all his shortcomings from our modern point of view, is that of the three Graces from the picture called "Primavera" (Pl. 20). It is flatter than many of his works, the indication of modelling being reduced to the lowest terms, but this is of no consequence whatever. In this kind of art the indication of modelling might be entirely eliminated, leaving the result as flat as Greek vase painting, with no detriment to the essential quality of it. There is no foreshortening, the avoidance of it in the complicated arrangement of the arms being very noticeable. Even the feet are not foreshortened, and, in one of the figures, the toes are turned out beyond the possibility of nature in the effort to avoid this difficulty. But study this lovely arrangement of lovely lines; learn, if you can, to appreciate their flow, their subtlety, their vitality, and inimitable grace, the sense of movement and of life that they convey; observe the delicate stiffness, as of flower-stalks, in the lines of the figures, the swiftness, as of living flame, in the curves of hair or filmy drapery; feel the passionate intensity of the artist, controlled by rigid discipline and refined taste, as his hand follows in its daintiest modulations and finest contrasts this melody of pure line— then you may begin to understand why he is the greatest master of linear drawing in our Western art. For myself, I should rate him the greatest in all art, placing him above even the best that China and Japan have done in a branch of art in which China and Japan have always excelled.

The drawing of Michelangelo is entirely different from this. He came at the end of a long succession of artists who had striven to master the significance of the human figure, and he resumed everything they had learned. He is almost too fond of foreshortening, using it sometimes, one suspects, merely to display his mastery of it; and his drawing is so far from flat that it depends more on modelling and on interior markings than on the contour. He is a draughtsman, not a chiaroscurist or a colorist, therefore he does not drown his forms in light and shadow or lose his edges in the mystery of atmosphere, but you may see many a drawing of his in which the form is hatched into existence with pen or crayon lines like the strokes of a sculptor's chisel, everything being determined except the final outline. He cared little for mere correctness, indulging in any exaggeration that would enhance the sense of bulk and structure which he wished to convey, and the habit of exaggeration grew upon him while the restraint of direct study from nature operated less and less, so that in his latest paintings the human figure becomes swollen into something almost monstrous, however titanic in its expression of energy. To have him at his best you must take him not only before the "Last Judgment" but before the Prophets and Sibyls—you must take him in the great central panels of the Sistine Ceiling. There, in such a composition as the "Creation of Adam" (Pl. 21), you have the highest reach of constructive figure drawing, as in the "Primavera" you have the standard of pure linear expression.

There is magnificent line in this fresco, also, the sweeping movement of the Creator and his attendant spirits being attained in the only way in which motion ever has been attained in painting—by composition of line. But all that can be told by line—even the difference between the energetic, pointing finger of the Almighty and the limp hand of the half-awakened Adam—is subordinate to the realization of these two figures as solid objects in space, to the expression of their structure as human bodies made of bone and muscle, and of the stresses and interactions of these bones and muscles as affected by position and movement. What particularly concerned Michelangelo was the roll of Adam's mighty thorax upon his pelvis; the forcing upward of his right shoulder on which his weight rests, and the elongation of the left pectoral by the stretching of the arm; the strain on the muscles of the neck caused by the turn of

Plate 17.—"Madame Rivière," by Ingres.

In the Louvre.

the head, and the swelling and flattening
of thigh and calf in the bent leg. As an
ideal yet real presentation of the human
figure, magnificently explicit in the rendering of all significant detail, but from
which everything accidental or insignificant has been purged away, there is nothing like this in painting, and nothing in
any art except the sublime figures from
the pediment of the Parthenon.

But why all this interest in the human
body? Well, in the first place, because
the great figure artists are made so, and
nothing else seems to them so beautiful
or so significant. And because meanings
and intentions can be conveyed by figure
drawing that can be conveyed in no other
way. These movements and stresses of
the figure communicate themselves to
you, and you feel them in your own body,
thereby attaining a sense of power and
freedom you are never likely to get from
anything else; and they put you into the

mood of the being who displays them and make you, by the state of the body, divine the state of the soul. For, in the hands of a master, the body is infinitely more expressive than the face, and the art of figure drawing is one of the most intellectual and expressional of the arts.

All drawing proceeds in one or both of these two ways, yet the drawing of Rembrandt seems, at first, to proceed by neither. In his paintings everything is so drenched in light and shade that both drawing and color almost cease to exist. His manner of drawing is better studied in his etchings or in his sketches in pen or crayon. It is a very personal manner, as is everything else about this extremely personal and romantic artist. He seems to care nothing about line for its own sake, and one cannot imagine his arranging a bouquet of beautiful lines as Botticelli would do. He seems to care even less for pure form, and his studies of the nude are misshapen, ill-articulated, hideous in the extreme. Yet with an extraordinarily sure instinct he selects so much of line as shall convey a sense of movement, so much of form as shall suggest a mental state, while with every touch he is implying the light and shade that shall afterward envelop the whole. In the hands of the great genius who invented it, this kind of drawing is amazingly expressive. With the merest shorthand of blots and scratches he makes you understand just what his characters are doing and how they are feeling —he can show you, for instance, the lamenting of Lot (Pl. 22) as he leaves his home under the guidance of the earnest angel, the sadness of the daughters and the unconcern of the maids, even the angry unreconcilableness of Lot's wife, who does not wish to go and will surely look back. In his hands such drawing may be called the drawing of spiritual significance; but, like all romantic and personal geniuses, Rembrandt is a bad model, and his method, in the hands of lesser men, becomes little more than picturesque draughtsmanship—the drawing of effect, rather than of form, of the accidental rather than of the essential— a lower kind than any other except the merely academic or the merely naturalistic and photographic.

The sense of pure line being nearly the rarest gift of our Western artists, most of the drawing our art has produced has been rather of the Michelangelesque type than of the Botticellian, and a great deal of it has been directly descended from Michelangelo himself. Raphael, the great designer and decorator, modified Michelangelo's drawing to suit his decorative purpose and passed on his modification as the model of academic draughtsmanship. His line is not particularly living, his structure not especially realized, but his drawing is admirably suited to its rôle in his

design, attracting no attention to itself
and allowing full play to the decorative
effect of the whole. His followers imitated
it, without having the qualities that ex-
cused it, and produced an empty and un-
interesting thing which, under the authority of his great name, they long imposed
on the world.

The Venetians simplified drawing for the
sake of color as Raphael simplified it for
the sake of decorative effect. To them the
detailed rendering of anatomical forms
was of less importance than the broad
glow of lighted flesh, and they amplified
the forms and omitted the accents to attain that breadth of effect which is one
of the conditions of the finest color. Yet
they were by no means the poor draughtsmen that they have generally been considered. Even in Titian there are great
beauties of form side by side with negli-
gences and weaknesses. Tintoretto's drawing was somewhat too schematic and

diagrammatical but, colorist and chiaroscurist as he was, he had an extraordinary sense of swift and expressive line and is one of the great masters of movement. Indeed his weakness is to have too much movement, his figures darting and tumbling about until one longs for a little stability and repose. As for Veronese, at his best, his drawing, in its large and simple masses, is almost as fine as any one's. His amplified forms are yet nobly structural, his strong sense of movement is controlled by a fine decorative placidity, his types are elevated yet full of character directly observed from nature. By taking the structural drawing of Michelangelo and broadening and simplifying it for the sake of color and decorative effect he has arrived at something very like the Greek conception of form, and it would be hard to find in modern art anything more essentially classic than the drawing of such figures as the Venus in the picture (Pl. 23)

Plate 18.—"Dance of the Nymphs," by Corot.

In the Louvre.

now in the Metropolitan Museum of New York—an antique torso transformed to palpitating flesh and blood.

Meanwhile the direct followers of Michelangelo, much less intelligent, had exaggerated his exaggerations, without understanding his meaning, and had created the baroque style of Pontormo and Daniele de Volterra, on which, and on direct study of the great master, Rubens founded his style of drawing. For there is no greater illusion than the commonly held idea that Rubens's drawing was what it was because he painted baggy Flemish women; and to hold his models responsible for what he did from them would be as unjust to Helena Fourment as a similar assumption in the case of Rembrandt would be libelous on poor Hendrickje Stopfels. No, Rubens's manner was deliberately adopted and reflected an ideal, however little it appeals to us, as firmly and consciously held as that of Michelangelo or that of Raphael. His drawing was developed from that of Michelangelo in the same way as his composition was developed from that of the Venetians, by giving greater luxuriance to the curves and by an especial accentuation of the double curve. His drawing, like his composition, is made up of S's, and to a critic who found fault with the bandy legs of one of his figures he replied with a calm demonstration that this line was in accord with all tradition. His style is neither naturalistic nor personal and romantic, but essentially classic and traditional. His florid and somewhat flaccid line is characteristic of the whole baroque period, and, somewhat weakened and prettified, becomes the keynote of the rococo also and of the draughtsmanship of Boucher and Fragonard (Pl. 24). The simpering shepherdesses of the Frenchmen are unlike enough to the overabundant nymphs and goddesses of the robust Fleming, but while the type has grown anæmic and slender, the line has become even more flowing and decidedly less functional.

It was against this overblown and somewhat decadent art that David directed his revolution. Unfortunately his effort for a purer taste only led him to a lifeless imitation of second-rate antique sculpture, not to any really vital or expressive drawing, while he succeeded only too well in destroying the old sense of color and the old mastery of technique. One of his earliest successes, the cold and pompous "Oath of the Horatii" (Pl. 25), remains the best he could do—his later work is still colder and more empty. Among the artists of the age of pseudo-classicism which David inaugurated there was but one real classicist, and that one was the only one who escaped from David's influence and was long treated with contempt and neglect. Prudhon's manner of painting was founded on Correggio, his conception of form was, what David's was not, truly Greek. He was a master of pure and beautiful line, and, consequently, of the suggestion of motion—he was, above all, a master of large and simple masses and of delicate and subtle modelling. His types are not heroic like those of the great Venetians, but, since the great Venetians, there has been nothing lovelier than the recumbent torso of his Psyche (Pl. 26), and perhaps there has been nowhere in painting anything more imbued with the spirit of the lighter art of the antique world.

Since Prudhon, there have been but two great draughtsmen, Ingres and Millet, and these two are of radically different types: Ingres the master of line and of pure beauty, Millet the master of mass and of expression.

The drawing of Ingres is not especially structural. He who has been called "The impeccable draughtsman" is by no means without faults of articulation, and even when he is correct in his expression of structure and function he is not particularly interested in these things. It is, above all, the line itself that interests him—the line in its own beauty and for its own character. Yet he has little of the feeling for movement of such a master as Botticelli—his line does not dance or flow. He seldom attempts action in his figures, and is not very successful when he does attempt it. His line is static, and what he expresses, by choice, is repose—a repose so fixed that it seems eternal. His "Source" will stand so forever while the water from her urn trickles through her fingers—his "Odalisque" (Pl. 27) will lie forever on her cushions, scarce breathing lest a breath disturb her reverie. In his portraits there is something of the passionate precision of Holbein, and the apparent coldness of his studies of the nude is the coldness of intense concentration, colorless because white hot. If his contours are fixed and rigid—frozen, as it were, into immobility —it is because only so could their infinite subtlety and beauty be displayed. If the "Odalisque" had one particle more possibility of movement you could never perceive how wonderful are those long curves of back and arms, how slight the variations of direction that mark the junctures of the muscles or the transitions from the bony to the fleshy planes. Like his composition, his drawing is set for all time into a crystalline perfection. There was never anything like it before, there can never be anything like it again. It is unique and incomparable, like the design of Raphael or the grandeur of Michelangelo.

The drawing of Millet, on the other hand, is little concerned with pure line; it occupies itself with bulk and action, with the expression of bodily strains and tensions and the resistance to weights. It is descended from the drawing of Michelangelo, and is the most effective drawing of this

Plate 19.—"The Gulf Stream," by Winslow Homer.
Property of the Metropolitan Museum of Art.

kind since that of the great Florentine, but it proceeds differently. Millet's figures are generally clothed, and could not show Michelangelo's particularity of articulation, even if their creator desired them to do so. But in his drawing, as in his composition and his way of telling a story, Millet remains the great eliminator. He never worked from nature, but he observed a given action again and again, drew it over and over until he had mastered what was essential in it, gave that essence with supreme force and clearness and gave nothing else. More than any other artist since the great Greek sculptors he achieved the typical, so that an action once studied by him is given its true and eternal expression and is not to be done again. His sower is *The* Sower, now and forever, and his "Woman Drawing Water" carries her buckets as buckets have been and must be carried since the beginning of the world.

How constantly he was preoccupied with
the exact notation of a weight, and the
amount of resistance determined by it,
may be shown by many passages in his
letters. You have heard how anxious he
was that his "Woman Drawing Water"
should "look as if she were carrying neither more nor less than the weight of the
buckets full of water." In the exact expression of this weight by the tension of
the arms and the dragging down of the
shoulders, in the erectness of the body between its equal burdens, in the slow and
shuffling walk enforced by the action, he
has achieved a monumental majesty; and
his figure looks as permanent as an
Egyptian colossus. But hear him again,
explaining the picture in the Chicago Art
Institute, "The New-born Calf." "The
expression of two men carrying a load
on a litter," he says, "naturally depends
on the weight which rests upon their
arms . . . this simple fact is the whole

reason of the . . . solemnity" which his detractors thought absurd but which is, in truth, the great merit of the picture. It is the logical and inevitable result of a large and typical rendering of the action, and Millet made his two peasants carry the calf, "as if it were the Ark of the Covenant" because that is the way men do carry a weight. He could even give to a man wheeling a barrow-load of dung (Pl. 28) all the solemnity and grandeur of style of one of Michelangelo's prophets.

Millet and Ingres are, in their several ways, capital examples of what great drawing is. For examples of what it is not one may go to almost any of their successors. Since Millet a hundred artists have painted peasants, but, for lack of his large comprehension of form, they have produced nothing but trivial anecdotes, or sentimentalities, or snapshot photographs of accidental and momentary conditions. Since Ingres a hundred artists have tried to continue the traditions of the school, but have produced nothing better than the academic literalism of Gérôme or the sweet insipidity of Bougereau. The drawing of Bougereau, with its superficial correctness and its entire lack of functional expression; with its hands which never grasp anything and its feet which never support any weight; with its apparent idealization which amounts to no more than the prettifying of studio models— this is the drawing most trying to the soul of any one capable of understanding what real draughtsmanship is; yet it is precisely this drawing that people will persist in supposing the thing desired by those of us who raise our voices against the formlessness of impressionism.

Almost all the drawing of the mid-nineteenth century was sheer naturalism and so is the larger part of what we still have. With the exception of Baudry, who had a real feeling for structure and action,

and of Leighton, who sometimes achieved
a large nobility of type, most of the academic painters did little more than clothe
an accurate transcript of ordinary nature
with a certain specious elegance, while
the non-academic painters only left out
the elegance. For the students of light and
color drawing became but a disagreeable
necessity, as for the virtuosi it is a mere
regulation of the shapes and sizes of the
brush strokes with which all things are
represented. In this country we have, in
George De Forest Brush, a lover of the
line, and among our mural painters one
or two have tried to attain to style. But,
for the most part, the conception of drawing as anything more than the accurate
placing of things has disappeared.

Against this literalism there was bound
to be a reaction, but when it came it did
not take the form either of the significant
draughtsmanship of Michelangelo and Millet or the linear beauty of Botticelli and

Ingres. It began with Puvis de Chavannes and took the form of a decorative simplification of the figure in the line of that adopted by Raphael, but gradually pushed much further. In the earlier work of Puvis there are figures of great beauty that Raphael himself might not have disowned—figures in which the simplification of natural forms has proceeded no further than to give a certain dignity of style and to elevate the result above the mere imitation of a given model. Such figures as those in the mural painting at Amiens called "Rest" (Pl. 29) are beautiful examples of what decorative draughtsmanship should be, the variation from nature being just sufficient to avoid the literal and to fit them for their rôle in a poetic and decorative composition. But the austerity of Puvis's temper was not satisfied and, in later work, we find him emulating the primitive painters of Italy, drawing figures that resemble those of Giotto in their blocky simplicity,

[148]

and attaining thereby something of Giotto's architectural solemnity of effect. In
his latest work he seems to me to lose his
grip on drawing altogether and to produce
figures that are out of joint and wrongly
put together, or that cease to be figures at
all and become mere spaces of pinkish
color (Pl. 30). His feeling for arrangement and spacing and his use of a beautiful if limited color scheme still save him,
and he remains a decorator; but he has
ceased to be a draughtsman.

The only credible account I have seen of
some of the latest aberrations of modern
art is that they are an attempt to carry still
farther what Puvis had already carried too
far: to bring about the entire disassociation
of abstract line and mass from representation; to make art altogether "subjective,"
reflecting nothing but the whim of the
artist and having no connection, except
in the artist's consciousness, with anything outside itself. For models we are to

go back of Giotto and even of the Byzantines, and found our practice on that of savage peoples, Hottentots, or Alaskan Indians, and by way of remedying the evils of too much naturalism we are to destroy altogether what the world has loved as art. In the hands of young Parisian students, bitten by the desire of notoriety, this programme has produced results unspeakable and almost unbelievable, more hideous, morally and materially, than any of the savage art it emulates.

It is root and branch work, certainly, but this short method with naturalism will not answer. The remedy is far worse than the disease. It is time that the Classic Spirit should protest, in the name of right reason, that if art is not a mere imitation of nature no more is it sheer irresponsibility and the unregulated exploitation of individuality. The art of painting is an art of arrangement of lines, spaces, and colors which shall express the artist's

Plate 20.—"The Three Graces" (Primavera), by Botticelli.

In the Academy, Florence.

mind while suggesting and recalling the aspects of nature; and if it is not art without that arrangement which removes it from literalism, it is not painting without such degree of imitation as shall give the necessary suggestion. In the most perfect works of art the expressive and the imitative elements are so intimately combined that it is impossible to separate them, and one knows not whether the work is more admirable for its beauty and expressiveness or for its truth. In inferior works the one or the other character predominates, but if both are not present in some considerable degree the work ceases to be of any importance. Of the two extremes, the self-abandonment to mere expression is the more dangerous, for that way lie eccentricity and madness; and the most prosaic picture ever painted by the most prosaic Dutchman is far more like the greatest art than is the rabid self-exploitation of these modern savages.

I should not have felt it necessary to treat this, so-called, post-impressionist movement with any seriousness—feeling sure that the mere flight of time must settle its business, and that without long delay—were it not that, at the present moment, a number of critics, some of whom have earned by intelligent work the right to be heard, are trying to convince themselves and the public that it is vital and important. With some of them their state of mind seems to be the result of long occupation with primitive art, which has so accustomed them to finding beauty of line or mass where there is little naturalism that they cannot see these qualities where they are combined with a knowledge of nature. They imagine that Matisse and his followers have rediscovered the line because there is evidently nothing else in their work; forgetting that the great and really difficult task is to draw beautifully and expressively without drawing falsely, and that it is of no advantage to the abstract beauty of a figure that its joints should bend the wrong way, or that it should have no joints at all but resemble something between a block of wood and a jelly-fish.

For others there is no such excuse, and one can only imagine that they are frightened by the long series of critical blunders that has marked the nineteenth century, and are determined, this time, not to be caught napping. Nearly all our greatest painters—and some that are, perhaps, not quite so great as we are just now inclined to think them—have been first misunderstood and abused as mere eccentrics. It was so with Millet and with Corot, it was so with Monet and Whistler; and in each case the unhappy critics had to reverse themselves and, in some cases, to swing to the other extreme and over-praise as they had overblamed. Here is a set of men whose art is so crazy that anything which formerly seemed eccentric pales to bourgeois commonplace in the comparison. What so natural as to assume that these, too, are great men, and to take the inevitable step at once, and as gracefully as possible? Their only answer to criticism is to assume an attitude of superiority and to say, smilingly and condescendingly, "Of course *you* could not be expected to understand." Let us hasten to show that we are not so stupid as our brothers of the past. If we do not understand either, at least we can exercise the virtue of faith, which has been defined as believing what one knows to be untrue.

In the tales of Hans Christian Andersen one may read how a certain monarch was supposed to be possessed of a suit of clothes of extraordinary richness and beauty but quite invisible to all unintelligent and stupid people. The King himself had never seen them, but as long as others believed in their existence he kept his mouth shut and received with complacence the glory which came to him as their possessor. The Prime Minister and the Lord Chamberlain and the members of the Privy Council were all equally blind to these wonderful garments, but each thought the others saw them, and so they joined in a chorus of praises, lauding the magnificence of the stuff, the splendor of the embroidery, and the perfection of the cut. Even the little page boys solemnly gathered up nothing, and pretended to carry the tails of the robe which they thought must certainly be there if only they were bright enough to see it. At last it was determined that his Majesty should walk in public procession through his capital, that every one might have an opportunity to behold the wonderful clothes. There were heralds and trumpeters, making a great noise with their trumpets, and knights and men at arms and judges and clergy, and, at last, under a canopy, the King himself, walking very grandly with his head in air and followed by the three pages that bore the invisible train. And the people all rubbed their eyes and each one said to himself, "Dear me! Am I so stupid? I really can't see anything"; and then they all shouted, "Long live the King and his incomparable clothes!" But presently the procession passed by a place where there stood a tiny boy in the street; and the boy, not being old enough to know better and, perhaps, not having been well brought up, spoke right out in a loud voice, saying: "But he hasn't got anything on!" And then— well, then every one suddenly saw that his Majesty was walking through the streets in his shirt.

Now it may be my own lack of intelligence that prevents my seeing the wonderful garment of art worn by some of the latest exponents of modernism. The rich stuff and the splendid embroidery, which others assure me they see, may really be

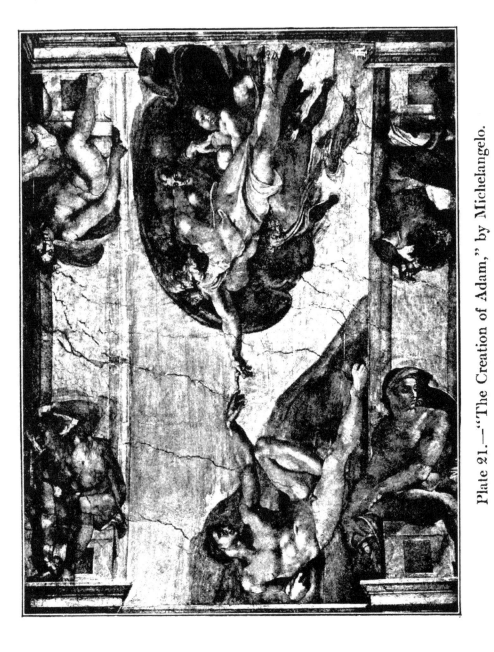

Plate 21.—"The Creation of Adam," by Michelangelo.

In the Sistine Chapel.

there and I may be too blind or too stupid to perceive it. But if the gods made me stupid it rests with myself to be honest; and so I can only cry, with the little boy in the street: "They have nothing on! They have nothing on!"

Homer and Rembrant did not
use intense color palette

V

LIGHT AND SHADE AND COLOR

The several elements of the art of painting are so intertwined, and run into and
out of each other in so complex a manner,
that it is very difficult to deal with any one
of them separately and without reference
to the others. One cannot speak of the
treatment of the subject without reference
to design, or of design without reference
to drawing; still less can one separate the
consideration of light and shade from that
of color, for, in painting of any ripeness of
development, each of these elements is
profoundly modified by the other. They
are, as it were, the warp and woof of a
united texture which overlies and en-
riches the structure of design. And, again,
the very words light and shade mean a
number of different things for which we

need, but have not, clearly differentiated terms. The vocabulary of our language, in matters of art, is singularly limited; and, while it has been somewhat enriched of recent years, it has also been confused by using old words in new senses, so that we are little better off than before. Perhaps we can best begin by separating light and shade into three forms which, however, more or less overlap and run into each other and can seldom be entirely separated. We shall call them light and dark, which is an element of design; modelling, which is an element of drawing; and light and shadow, or true chiaroscuro, which is a nearly independent element of painting and tends in its fullest development to obscure or obliterate all the others.

You have light and dark, in its simplest form, in Greek vase painting, in which there are either light figures on a dark ground or dark figures on a light ground, the division into light and dark being merely an accentuation of the primary division into filled and empty spaces and having nothing to do with light and shadow or even with modelling. But if, instead of working in two tones, the artist works in polychromy, it is evident that, without any modelling or light and shadow, he may have as many different degrees of light and dark as there are different colors in his scheme, each color having its own place in a scale of light and dark without regard to its special quality as color. Here we approach the old and best sense of that much abused word "values," which has come to mean so many things that it now means next to nothing. As Fromentin used it, it signified the degree of light or dark, on a scale from black to white, of any object in a picture, considered as a whole, without regard to its own light and shade. Now, into this painting in flat colors, which have

[160]

their necessary values, you may introduce
a certain amount of that light and shade
which makes modelling without altering
the essential nature of your work, each
space of color retaining its complete individuality as a space of blue or white or
red and its own value in the scale of light
and dark, the lights and shades within
its boundaries being quite subordinate.
This is the usual condition in primitive
painting and is the condition to which, as
we shall see, classic and, especially, decorative painting tends, for several reasons,
to return. But if, in the desire to procure
the illusion of solidity and of the existence
of figures or objects in free space, you
push the degree of light and shade in
individual objects much further, an entirely new condition results. The difference between the light and the shadow
on a given object may become greater
than the difference between the value of
that object as a whole and that of another

object near it, and the lights of the two objects are bound together as light and their shadows as shade. The result is a new pattern, overlying and cutting across the original linear pattern, and more or less independent of it. In its fullest development this true light and shadow becomes so predominant that the original linear pattern ceases to have any importance and the original scheme of separate or local colors is absorbed in the color, whether warm or cold, of the light, and the contrasting color of the shadow. Finally, as distance and open air are attempted, all colors, all values, and all light and shade are modified by atmosphere and the influence of the sky, color and chiaroscuro mingle and confound their identities, and dance from end to end of the canvas transcending all bounds and absorbing everything into themselves.

It is late in the history of painting before light and shade progresses beyond the

Plate 22.—"Lot and His Family," from a drawing by Rembrandt.
In the Lenox Library, N. Y.

stage of modelling. Leonardo da Vinci has always been considered an innovator in light and shade, and a great chiaroscurist, yet he did little more than complete the modelling of his figures, making them look like figures in the round where earlier men had been contented with figures in relief. Both Michelangelo and Raphael were contented to rest here, and so, for the most part, were their followers and imitators. Even much later, painters like Caravaggio and Ribera—the tenebrists, as they were called—only darkened the shadows to blackness, exaggerating and vulgarizing their modelling without substituting light and shadow for it as a distinct element of expression. The first painters to use light and shadow, in its fullness, as an overlying pattern, independent of the linear pattern under it, were Correggio and the Venetians; and even with them the original linear pattern maintains its importance, so that an outline drawing of one of their pictures always gives an idea of the essential nature of the design, though it robs it of its richness. With Rembrandt we reach the stage of fully developed chiaroscuro absorbing or overriding everything else, so that an outline drawing of one of his compositions is almost inconceivable and, if attempted, would give no idea of the real picture because omitting the thing on which he principally relies for his effect.

In the hands of its especial masters light and shade is a powerful means of poetic and imaginative expression. With Correggio (Pl. 31) the glow of light on a shoulder or a bosom, the soft veil of shadow on a woman's side, act as mitigants to a too voluptuous ideal, and remove his creations into a realm of dreamy enjoyment where is no conscience and no responsibility— nothing but an endless lotus-eating calm. With the tempestuous Tintoretto everything is changed. Light and shade be-

comes lurid, fantastic, full of wild energy.
He bars his figures with unexpected and,
sometimes, unaccountable cast shadows;
his light comes from anywhere and nowhere and brings out a head or arm into
sharp relief and throws a body into deep
shadow. His original design is crossed and
recrossed by another one of light and
darkness which everywhere contradicts it
and yet greatly enhances its effect. With
Rembrandt light and shadow become the
only things of consequence, and express,
as nothing else could, his strangely poetic
mind. With them he can reveal the spiritual and create the supernatural, he can
place you in presence of a miracle or make
you see the human soul.

One of the most acute of present-day
critics* has maintained, in a recent book,
that the art of imaginative design is dependent on the use of contours and the
avoidance of "chiaroscuro and modelling

* Bernard Berenson. A Sienese Painter of the Francis-
can Legend, Dent., 1909.

in the round," because modelling "never allows us to forget our bodies." It seems to me that Mr. Berenson's exclusive devotion to Italian art has made him strangely forgetful of Rembrandt, and that his error is also, in part, due to a confusion of two things which, as I have tried to show, are essentially different: modelling and true chiaroscuro. Modelling does, indeed, insist upon the body—true chiaroscuro conceals it. In its fully developed form, light and shadow becomes mystery, absorbs substance as well as line, and becomes the one means for the expression of the otherwise inexpressible. It is not in the work of any Sienese linealist, nor even in the work of any Oriental, that religious emotion and the awe of the supernatural have been most truly translated into the terms of art; it is in the painting of "The Supper at Emaus" and the etching of "Dr. Faustus" (Pl. 32).

But just because light and shade is so

mysterious and so absorbing, because
it tends to take the place of design and
drawing and even color, it is a dangerous
tool. It requires a great imaginative genius
to make what it gives us a fair exchange
for what it takes away. In the hands of
smaller men than Rembrandt—and even
in his when, for the moment, his imagination is in abeyance—it degenerates into a
rather paltry picturesqueness—an insistence on the accident of lighting rather
than on the nature of the thing lighted.
The true lover of either form or color will
always keep it in subordination to other
things, using it as an ornament to his
work, not as the substance of it.

Even after Rembrandt there was one
more step for light and shade to take, and
that step it took in the latter part of the
nineteenth century. That step was to
unite itself with color so that the two were
no longer distinguishable, to bend both
to the rendering of natural light in the

open air, and to make light the only real subject of painting, the objects which reflect it being no longer of any individual interest. The impressionist movement, which effected this step, was undoubtedly of some service, and the step itself was, to some extent, an advance. It brought back into art the element of color when that element was sadly needed, for most modern color, through exact imitation of studio effects and through the decay of technical knowledge, had become cold and muddy; and it discovered things about natural effects of light which may prove useful to future masters who shall have thoroughly assimilated them and can employ them without undue insistence on their importance. Its great defect was its neglect of art; for color, even more than drawing, requires that art shall control the study of nature, and that things shall be done for the purpose of expression, not merely for the love of imitation.

But even as science, impressionism was not wholly new. Its greatest discoveries are supposed to be the colored shadow, especially the blue or violet shadow, and the use of broken color instead of united tones. In both of these discoveries it had been anticipated. Leonardo shows us, in his note-books, that he had not only observed the blue shadow but was perfectly aware of its reason, and he has written long passages of description of natural effects that are as acute in observation of the action of light and atmosphere as if they were the work of a painter of to-day. The colored shadow and the broken tone were the common property of all good colorists, the only difference between the best of the old work and the best of the new, in that respect, being that the old painters were more particular that their method of securing the broken tone should not be obvious and should not interfere with the beauty of their surfaces. And the blue shadow itself had been painted by Vermeer. Indeed this extraordinary painter had anticipated many of the most modern devices for representing light and atmosphere, including that manner of painting in minute dots which has been given the name of pointillism.

Leonardo not only gives us his observations of natural effects—he gives us his reason for not using them in his art. There are several long passages among his notes describing the effects of foliage as seen by transmitted and reflected light, in which the blue surface lights, the yellowness of transparent leaves seen from below, and the mottling of these leaves by the shadows of other leaves which come between them and the sun, are considered with great particularity. And then comes this warning: "Never represent leaves as though transparent in the sun, *because they are always indistinct.*" And again: "The structure of such a leaf is indis-

Plate 23.—"Venus and Mars Bound by Cupid," by Veronese.

Property of the Metropolitan Museum of Art.

tinct, and the imitation of it is to be avoided." There speaks the true classic spirit. The structure is indistinct, and no amount of illusion will compensate, to the true classicist, for the lack of clarity and for the lack of structure. Impressionism, which makes light its only subject, and ruthlessly sacrifices clarity and structure in the interest of illusion, is acceptable in inverse proportion to the essential beauty and interest of the objects represented. It may be admirable in still-life, where no one cares about the objects themselves. They are glorified by the light rather than made insignificant by it. It is not for nothing that so many of the best canvases of the moderns are pictures of still-life, and it is the modern study of light and color for its own sake that is responsible for the doctrine that still-life is as good a subject for art as any other. It is, indeed, a better subject than any other for this kind of art, for it entails less loss

to set against the gain. In the treatment
of landscape impressionism may still be
tolerable, because light naturally plays
a great rôle in landscape painting; but
no painter who cares for the anatomy of
earth or the growth and life of trees will
ever be quite satisfied with it. In figure
painting it is intolerable. In its hands the
human figure, the most beautiful and the
most interesting thing in all the world, is
merged in the landscape, as the landscape
itself is lost in the light that falls upon it,
and man himself becomes no more than
an accident among other accidents. If
Leonardo could not bring himself to paint
a leaf "transparent in the sun," what
would he have said to some of our modern
pictures in which the glorious human
body, that miracle of nature, becomes no
more than a surface on which the pattern
of the leaf-shadows may trace itself
as on a smooth stone? Still less could he
have endured to see it made a lay figure

for the study of cross lights, red on one side and blue on the other as if it stood between a chemist's bottles.

But if modern literalism has produced colorlessness, so that a modern gallery seems filled with chalky and muddy and blackish pictures, from which the splendor and the subtlety of true color are alike absent; if the impressionistic study of color has obliterated form and structure without attaining the fullness of decorative beauty; yet the way out is not by following the post-impressionists into the denial of all connection with nature and the erecting of subjective emotion as the only standard. In color, as in form, we come back to the fundamental truth that painting is a representative art, and that while its version of nature is a heightened and glorified one it is not a denial of natural law. In its greatest magnificence we yet demand of color that it shall give us an illusion of truth; we ask of it that its variations from the actual shall not be perceived—indeed that they shall serve to heighten the sense of reality. To paint trees red and grass purple may be good heraldry, but such fancies have no other place in the art of painting than that of the blue boars and the green lions that used to decorate the signs of way-side inns.

Nor does this demand for a certain conformity to nature in itself impose any great privation upon the artist. If he needs a note of red, for the completion of his color-harmony or the expression of his emotion, he has only to introduce into his picture some object which may conceivably be red. If he wants a green or blue or purple it is not impossible to find objects of those colors. One of the great uses of drapery to the painter is that it allows of the introduction of any desired color into the general harmony of colors. But this sort of conformity to nature in the local color of objects introduced, while it may be sufficient for painting of a very primitive kind, is only the beginning of the conformities imposed upon painting of a more fully developed order. We must have, also, some sufficient recognition of the laws of light, some knowledge of the relation of the color of lights to the color of shadows. We must have, above all, a structure of light and dark, or of light and shade, underlying our color if we would prevent our color from being merely chaotic and elevate it to the plane of true decoration. As every color has its value as light or dark there will necessarily be some arrangement of light and dark accompanying any scheme of colors, but if the colors are selected and arranged for their quality as color only, leaving their effect as light and dark out of the account, that arrangement will be hap-hazard and therefore bad. It is necessary to weigh each particle of color for its value as well as for its chromatic effect, whether this value is intrinsic in the color or is the effect of light and shade, and to see that the whole pattern of light and dark is as carefully and thoroughly organized as the pattern of color. It is for this reason that the term "values" has been so extended as to cover even the differences of light and dark caused by modelling, and it is for this reason that the study of values has come to be considered of such vast importance. The thing was equally important before it received its modern name, and it remains equally important whether the scheme of light and dark is naturalistic or decorative—whether it is copied from something seen or invented for its own beauty. It is his lack of a feeling for values—that lack of a sense for the amount of light or dark included in his colors, which permits him to make a sunset cloud darker than the sky it rests in— that makes the color of Turner so spectacular and unsatisfactory. It is, even

Plate 24.—"The Bathers," by Fragonard.

more than the lack of form, the lack of a sense for values that reduces the color of Monticelli to a sort of unmeaning gorgeousness.

The perfect union of color and of values —each smallest fragment of the picture fulfilling its double function as a step in the scale of light and dark and as a note in the harmony of colors—produces that great unifying influence in a picture which we know as tone; and I know of no more wonderful instance of perfect tone than that of the greatest work of the greatest of artists, who has yet been thought of as anything but a painter and a colorist —Michelangelo's ceiling of the Sistine Chapel. Here is a space to be painted which has been estimated at ten thousand square feet, and the design is said to contain three hundred and forty-three figures; yet this vast scheme, which had, moreover, from the conditions of fresco painting, to be executed a bit at a time and without retouching, is held together from end to end with a perfection of unity as great as that of a tiny canvas by Terborch or Metsu. And this effect is produced by most subtle and beautiful means. The whole central portion of the ceiling, with its stories of the Creation and the Fall of Man, is based upon a chord of gold and violet. The lights, which are mainly the illuminated masses of the flesh, are of a thousand tints of grayish yellow or pale orange; the darks, which are made by the draperies, are reddish violet; the gray blue of sky forms the general half-tone. Occasionally there is a blue drapery, but the lights of it are pale yellow, the local color subsisting only in the shadows. As you descend from this central portion to the pendentives and the lunettes the color grows richer and fuller; you have deep blues and greens and rich reds, but always there is the golden light modifying the local tones, the full-colored shadow look-

ing violaceous by reason of the contrast.
The effect of the whole is so rich, so
harmonious, so right in the relations of its
parts and in the relation of the whole to
its surroundings, so perfectly in air and
so lacking in heaviness, that, when I first
saw it, I forgot, for the time, the stupen-
dous design and marvellous draughtsmanship in admiration for its glory of color
and painter-like mastery of tone. Considering the overwhelming difficulty of
the task, I know of nothing else in the
world comparable to this as a display of
the highest powers of the colorist.

It is the perfect notation of values, the
union of the exact degree of light or dark
with the exact quality of warm or cold
color necessary to the place where it occurs,
which gives the sense of color to many a
picture of grayish or brownish tone in
which positive colors hardly exist. It is
this which makes the silvery grays of
Correggio's "Danaë" so lovely and so

colorful that they can confront even the glowing hues of Titian without fear. It is this which gives us the illusion of color in Rembrandt, even when he introduces nothing in his pictures but variations of golden brown. It is his mastery of values, even more than the intrinsic beauty of his cold hues, that makes Vermeer so precious. It is mastery of values that makes Corot, at his grayest, a master of color.

But it is not only such gray or brown pictures that possess tone—the richest and most splendid canvases of Titian and Giorgione possess it also, and in equal measure, and they possess it through this same double service of each particle of pigment as a part of a comprehensive scheme of color, and as a part of an equally comprehensive scheme of light and dark. This scheme of light and dark, which is the framework on which the color is woven, is in their works, to some extent, conventional and decorative rather

than strictly naturalistic. The flesh, for
instance, is almost always lighter than the
sky, which is the reverse of what usually
happens in the open air; and it is so in
order to give the human figure that dominance in the pictorial scheme which its life
and its importance to the mind give it
in our consciousness. It is one of those
cases, and there are many such in art,
where a convention produces the effect of
truth more completely than would an
exact compliance with the actual. But if
the values of these Venetian masterpieces
are not quite nature's values, they are
none the less profoundly studied; and as
every good Venetian picture has a linear
design that will retain its air of magnificent mastery when the composition is
stripped to its bare bones by old-fashioned
wood-engraving, so it has a muscular
structure of light and dark that is still consummate when photography has robbed
it of its colors. Put some of the later

pictures of Turner and most of the modern impressionistic works to the same test, and you will have little or nothing left. They have no blood and bone under the skin of surface beauty—their iridescence is that of a blown bladder.

Such grasp and knowledge of both light and shade and color as is necessary to the attainment of harmony by the way of true tone is difficult of acquisition, and it is not to be wondered at, human nature being what it is, that various short cuts to harmony have been attempted and various forms of false or artificial tone invented. It was the desire to attain to an artificial harmony, and to something that might answer for tone, without the necessity of too much thought or labor, that led to the once well-nigh universal use of bitumen. It used to be spread over the whole surface to be painted upon, and painted into while it was wet, so that it mixed itself in some degree with all the

Plate 25.—"The Oath of the Horatii," by David.

In the Louvre

colors on the canvas, acting as a sort of mechanical harmonizer and taking the place of knowledge in preventing false contrasts and crudity. This use of bitumen has been frequently lamented because of its impermanence—because it led to blackening and cracking and, in some cases, almost to the sliding off the canvas of the picture painted upon it. It seems to me truly lamentable because it was false art in the first place, and inevitably vitiated the color of the artists who indulged in it. It was easy—fatally easy— and art made easy is always art made bad.

The day of bitumen has passed—one of the last artists to base his work upon it was Munkacsy, whose pictures are fast blackening into invisibility upon the walls of our museums—and we might look upon our escape from it with some complacency were it not for the fact that other means of mechanical harmonizing are still employed. I do not know whether there are still any papers published of the sort which used, not so long ago, to give instructions to amateurs whereby they might produce works of art without any knowledge of nature. They used to contain recipes something like this: for the flesh use light red, yellow ochre and white with—here was the invariable part—with "a little ivory black to give it tone." It sounds naïve enough, put in that simple way, and yet that recipe of "a little ivory black" as a "universal harmonizer" was one of the things on which no less a person than James McNeill Whistler relied for the production of his delicate symphonies. In the hands of a hundred imitators and followers it has become almost the only thing relied on, and instead of a little ivory black it has become a good deal.

Take another instance. In the old bituminous days all shadows were brown, and the acceptance of that rule saved a

vast deal of trouble. Then the impressionists discovered that some shadows are
blue. The logical result should have been
a new impulse toward the thorough study
of the real color of shadows. The actual
result, in many cases, has been merely
to install blue instead of brown, as a
thought-saver and time-saver. "All shadows are blue," says the young painter
who thinks himself modern, and troubles
no more about them, but paints them blue
where they would, in nature, be brown or
orange or anything but blue. As a "universal harmonizer," if we are to have such
a thing, I confess to preferring bitumen,
for the warm tones of those days were
at least more agreeable to the eye than
the icy tones of these.

Finally, there is the harmony by attenua-
tion, the use of pale and faded colors, the
reign of universal half-tone, inaugurated
by Puvis de Chavannes. As he first used
it, in the decoration of cold, gray build-

ings, it was admirably suited to its purpose, and his dead tones seemed a part of
the stone and plaster that surrounded
them. In other situations it was not so
successful, even where he used it himself
—his decorations in the Boston Public
Library never seem to me to mate with the
yellow marble of that splendid interior—
and in the hands of others it became only
one more case of the universal harmonizer.
This time it was a little, or a good deal,
of white "to give it tone." As confession is
good for the soul, I may admit that the
influence of Puvis was so dominant, when
I began to have decorative commissions
to fill, that it carried me away, for a time,
into this harmonization by paleness. I
hope I have learned something since those
days, and if I had my two lunettes in the
Library of Congress to paint again the
result, whether better or worse, would be
something very different from the ghosts
of paintings I actually placed there.

All of these methods are really confessions of weakness—they are efforts to avoid difficulties instead of conquering them. The ideal is to paint with the full palette and, on occasion, with the full strength of the palette, and to harmonize the result by sheer knowledge: knowledge of the laws of light and shade; knowledge of the harmonies and contrasts of colors; knowledge of the relations of the color of light to the color of shadow. Nothing but long study will give a painter this knowledge. The laws of color cannot be written in any form precise enough to help him greatly. A competent master, if there were such, might greatly shorten the road for him by practical advice and demonstration, but even he could only start the student upon the right road. A natural gift is indispensable to begin with, but that will carry one no farther in color than it would in drawing. Years of work, years of discipline, years of observation of art and of nature—that is the only recipe. The only universal harmonizer is "brains, sir."

While it is true that good color is based upon a scheme of light and dark or light and shadow, and that true tone is only to be attained by a perfect adjustment of color to values, yet in proportion as color is the dominant preoccupation of the artist it manifests a tendency to assume the superior position and to relegate light and shade to the inferior place. It tends to revert toward the primitive condition, in which each space of color kept its own quality throughout, unsullied by shadows; and while it admits and relies upon light and shade it insists that this element shall be so subordinated that it shall never disguise the quality of a given color as color. However rich the variations within their borders, red must yet be red, from one end to the other, and blue, blue; and if there are a dozen different reds, scarlet and crimson and rose will be scarlet and crim-

Plate 26.—"L'Enlèvement de Psyché," by Prudhon.

In the Louvre.

son and rose through each variation of shadow and half-tone and high light and no one will be confusable with any other. This persistence of the local color through all conditions of light or shadow or reflection is a quality of all true colorists, but it is perhaps most astonishing in the work of Veronese and is one of the things that make him, on the whole, the most accomplished painter that ever lived. He can do anything with color or with light and shade, can throw whole figures into cast shadow, can reverberate reflections from one color to another, can strike a brilliant golden high light onto a mantle of violet silk; yet the true local color of each object is never in doubt. From the deepest shadow to the highest light it preserves its identity and is immediately distinguishable from every other color near it. What the primitives achieved by the omission of modulation he achieves with the fullest modulation.

In Veronese, also, you will find the best
example of another habit of the great
colorists which connects their practice
with that of the primitives. In primitive
painting a given color was shaded, in so
far as it was shaded at all, with more of
the same color, a blue drapery being
simply a little deeper blue in the shadows
than in the lights, and this method produced a crystalline purity of tint hard to
attain in any other manner. As chiaroscuro began to be studied this simple
manner was abandoned, shadows became
darker and heavier, and gradually absorbed all local colors, leaving them visible
only in the lights. But the colorists found
that all those things in nature which were
loveliest in color were colored in the
shadow rather than in the light. Look into
a rose and see how the color, which is so
faint as to be almost imperceptible on the
edges of the outer petals, grows deeper
and richer as you dive into its heart. Look

at the sky, on a clear day, and see how it is gradated from the pale horizon into a pure and ever purer blue as you approach the zenith. Look at a ruby and see how from the fiery high light it darkles into fuller and fuller red. This is the way that nature produces beautiful color, and this is the only way man has succeeded in producing it. The painter must know enough to modify this condition by such graying of cast shadows, such modulations of half-tones, as shall maintain the illusion of natural effect, but if he would give all the pleasure by his color that color is capable of giving he must, in the main, base his procedure on that of the primitives, coloring his shadows and attenuating his lights rather than coloring his lights and graying his shadows.

If the purity and beauty of individual hue is largely dependent on the subordination of light and shade and on this intensification of color in the shadow, it is also largely dependent on the technical method of painting. The most striking proof of this is found in comparing the coloring of our painters in water-color with that of our painters in oil. On going into an exhibition of water colors the first impression will be that the painters, good and bad, are all working in color. On going into an exhibition of oils the first impression is apt to be that every one is painting in mud or in chalk. It is not a question of the ability of the painters. Some of the water color painters are certain to be mediocre artists, and some of the oil painters are sure to be men of very great talent; yet in this one matter of beautiful and pure color the water colorists will maintain their advantage. What is even more conclusive, you will find the same man working in both mediums and producing clear and lovely results in the one and heavy opacity in the other. The contrast is no longer so striking as it used to be, because, alas, our water color painters are more and more abandoning the unique advantage of their material and imitating the muddiness of modern oil painting, but the contrast is still there.

In one of his lectures to the students of the Royal Academy, some years ago, Mr. George Clausen noticed this superior beauty of water color, and the reason for it, saying: "if you put a simple wash of color on paper it is always beautiful, because of its transparency." But he failed to draw what seems the natural conclusion from it. After some account of the ways in which the older painters secured an equivalent effect in oils, he goes on: "But these paths are outside the track of most artists to-day . . . we are more literal . . . we feel that it may be possible to paint with our first and main reference to nature as we see it around us and . . . to claim still that beauty of color may be found also in the plain aspect of visible

[193]

things." The real meaning of which is, that while splendid or lovely color has been secured in oil painting in the past and is secured in water color to-day, we must still go on muddling and missing it. Why must we? Having once admitted that a great part of the quality of fine color is dependent on transparency, why should we not go back to some one of the methods of the older painters by which transparency was secured?

There are several such methods which will call for consideration and be discussed, presently, in some detail. They are being studied, here and there, in this country, as are all the other problems of color. The late Louis Loeb was studying the use of glazes over a monochromatic foundation, and making great progress in the direction of rich and full color at the time of his death. A number of other American painters are pursuing similar investigations, and some of those that paint di-

[194]

Plate 27.—"Odalisque Couchée," by Ingres.

rectly, and without particular method, are constantly increasing the force and fulness of their palettes. They are still a small minority, but they are having their effect, and the walls of our exhibitions are yearly gaining in richness of color. I hope and believe that when the American school of painting is fully developed it will prove to be a school of colorists.

Cox likes Velesquez better
than Hals

VI

TECHNIQUE

Technique—I dislike the word but can
find no precise equivalent for it—is that
element of the art of painting which
has the least reliance upon the observation of nature. The subject of a picture
may be some place or event actually seen
by the artist; the design may be suggested
by something in nature or may even be
wholly copied from some felicitous natural arrangement; the drawing, the light
and shade, the coloring, however modified
by the artistic intention, must be more or
less imitative or representative. Nature
may decide for the artist what he shall
paint, but she has no voice in determining
how he shall paint it. The means at the
artist's disposal, the tools he uses and his

methods of employing them, are decided by the history and traditions of his art. On the purely technical side a piece of painting is good or bad as any other piece of craftsmanship is good or bad, according as it employs its tools and materials to the best advantage and for the intrinsic beauty of the material result, making a skin of oil paint as beautiful as it can be made.

But modern art has almost entirely lost the feeling for beautiful workmanship, as well as the knowledge of how to produce it. Of all the traditions of painting which were destroyed by the pseudo-classic revolution the technical tradition was the most thoroughly annihilated; and the modern artist has had to experiment and guess in the effort to rediscover the admirable methods of the older masters, or to muddle through without any method at all, relying upon the closeness of his observation of nature to take the place of any mastery of his materials. We have even so far forgotten what real technical beauty is, that if any man paints with a big brush and a certain swagger of handling we hail him, at once, as a master of technique, though every particle of his color may be muddy and heavy, though his rendering of form may be cursory and insufficient, though his canvases be unpleasant in their surface, though his pictures, from end to end, are but rough approximations to anything the painters of the past would have thought satisfactory. A parade of what we call "directness" and "frankness," and a "looseness" often not to be distinguished from slackness, have come to be almost the only technical qualities we admire.

This modern method of direct painting which has become wellnigh universal—a method in which everything, design, drawing, light and shade and color, is produced at once and with the fewest possible brush strokes—implies the assumption of a mastery little less than colossal. It is based, originally, upon the practice of two real masters, Velazquez and Frans Hals, but, it seems to me, upon a misreading of their work. Hals, at times, comes nearer to justifying modern practice than does Velazquez. He has the reputation of having been a hard drinker and there are pictures of his that look almost as if they might have been painted in a drunken frenzy, so meaningless and disorganized are his slashing brush strokes. There are also works painted late in life when, apparently, he had lost his skill of hand and almost his sureness of eye, which are fumbling and nearly formless, and which maintain their interest because of the vast acquired knowledge that the old man could not lose. But in the execution of Hals at his best, it is not his freedom that is most remarkable, it is his extraordinary precision.

Every touch is exactly right in shape and
position, in value and in color, to render
with utmost accuracy the object represented, whether it be a human head or a
bit of still-life. That these touches appear
to have been placed on the canvas at high
speed increases the wonder, but the wonder itself is in their certainty. If I had a
pupil who was bitten with the mania of
looseness, and was trying to run before
he could walk, I should like to place him
before one of the inimitable shooting-
guild pictures at Haarlaem and bid him
look at the character of the heads and
hands, at the clear distinction of bony and
fleshy planes, at the consummate naturalistic draughtsmanship; and I should say
to him: "When you can draw like that
we will talk of painting." I should ask
him to observe the rendering of the sword
hilts and halberds, of the dishes and
glasses, of the pattern on a cut-velvet
doublet, perfect in its repetition through

Plate 28.—"Peasant with Wheelbarrow," from the etching by Millet.

every inch of surface, absolute in its perspective as it runs in and out among the folds; and I should say to him: "when you can compass that precision, by any means, you may begin to attempt it with free touches." Then I should like to show him certain little panels by the same master, a few inches square, and make him see the beautiful, flowing, translucent pigment and ask him to produce one square inch of such a surface before he went further. Finally, I should take him to see that wonderful portrait of an old lady, belonging to Mr. Morgan, in the Metropolitan Museum and ask him to try to copy the indecipherable modelling of the head; to try to paint the ruff with its perfect simplicity and the entire regularity of its plaitings, in their proper foreshortenings, as they turn into the shadow; to make any approach to the quiet unity of light and color, the impeccable tone of the whole canvas. I think that, after a few such lessons, he

would be less content with what passes
for "technique" to-day.

As for Velazquez, his coolness and lucidity, his absolute freedom from ostentation
or any display of virtuosity, his seriousness and his completeness are among his
most obvious characteristics. Fortunately,
in his case, we have his early work and
can be sure—where, in the case of Hals,
we can only guess—by what steps he attained his ultimate mastery. There are
several of his quite early pictures in existence, little more than still-life studies, exercises in the representation of natural
facts and appearances. They are rather
hard, rather dull and commonplace,
closely studied and thoroughly finished,
the work of a good honest sudent, no
more. Then we have the early portraits,
simple in arrangement, quiet, almost
timid in execution, but fine in character
and beautiful in tone. It is only little by
little that he reaches the superb freedom

of the accomplished master. I should say to my hypothetical pupil: "begin where Velazquez began; take the steps he took; and, if you are able, we shall be glad to have you leave off where he left off."

But even in the hands of these masters the "direct method" of painting had its drawbacks as well as its virtues—was suited to some purposes and not to others. No man is great enough to carry on all the elements of painting at the same time and achieve equal and entire success in all. If design and drawing and color are to be attained with the one set of brush strokes, and without separate consideration, some or all of these elements will suffer. Neither Velazquez nor Hals was pre-eminently a designer; neither was, in the full sense, a colorist. Both were admirable draughtsmen as far as the correct placing and shaping of things is concerned, but neither of them had any conception of that higher drawing which is an intellectual art. Velazquez was the greater man of the two and comes nearer to attaining the great qualities of other schools. His "Surrender of Breda" is a nearly perfect composition for its purpose, but he could not succeed in another kind of art. His "Coronation of the Virgin," placed beside even a second-rate picture of the great Italian period, is commonplace both in the design and in the types and the manner of drawing. Hals hardly composed at all and his big portrait groups are put together anyhow. Velazquez, while he could not attain to the full beauty and glory of color, was a master of tone and even his largest works are admirably harmonized. Hals was capable of great beauty of color in passages, but his larger pictures are seldom quite perfectly in keeping. In his later days he abandoned color almost altogether and relied entirely upon the justness of his values to give effect to nearly monochromatic canvases. In a word, their methods were suited only to the purposes of an almost purely naturalistic art—an art occupying itself with the rendering of objects and effects immediately before the eye. And even so, there is one thing that to my mind, they could never perfectly render—the opaque color and the flowing or slashing stroke can never give quite the look of the human body, with its subtle modelling, its broad surfaces, its glowing lights and shadows, its peculiar irradiation and inner light. Correggio and Titian could render these qualities of flesh, not Velazquez or Hals.

It is, of course, precisely because Velazquez and Hals were so entirely naturalistic in temper that their methods have so influenced our naturalistic age. To a generation almost entirely absorbed in the effort to render the thing seen, their example could hardly fail to be decisive. But the example has been a very dangerous one. Even our most brilliant virtuosi have

never been able to combine the brilliancy
of these masters with their solidity and
sanity. In the hands of the rank and file
of modern painters the attempt has led
to lamentable results. The obsession of
the big brush has led to the attempt to
use it where a smaller one was obviously
called for, to the omission of all forms less
than an inch wide, and the reduction of
ears to jug handles and of the human face
to a diagram. The desire of freedom and
looseness has led to the stroke which is
slashing whether it is right or wrong and
which, in the worst examples, comes to
represent nothing but so much paint. The
attempt to do everything at once leads to
doing nothing well. We paint *at* the thing
rather than paint it, fail and repaint, often
without waiting for the first painting to
dry, make alterations, put darks where
lights were or lights where darks have
been, or lay one coat of practically the
same color over another. Where dark goes

Plate 29.—"Rest," by Puvis de Chavannes.

In Amiens.

over light the paint cracks. Where light goes over dark it becomes translucent, with time, and the dark becomes visible. Where the same color is twice laid the result is heaviness and muddiness. In our effort at what we mistakenly call technique we have forever lost all true technical beauty.

I do not think this is an over-strong statement of the faults of technical method in the average modern portrait or figure painting. Among the landscape painters, especially, though some figure painters practise it also, there is another kind of technique which seems to have come to us, directly, from the practice of Dupré, but of which the ultimate ancestor is Rembrandt—the technique of heavily loaded pigment and of extreme rugosity of surface. Rembrandt is the first master who ever used anything that we should now call heavy loading of paint, for the richest surfaces of the Venetians were only heavy enough for solidity. Rembrandt himself had an admirable thin technique which he applied when he was merely painting what he saw—the lucidity and beauty of surface in such a canvas as "The Gilder" is inimitable—and even in such a work as the wonderful "Orphan," in the Art Institute of Chicago, the loading is within bounds and the surface is all of a piece. But he had a love for glitter, which lead to heavily projecting high lights, and he needed rough surfaces to take his glazes. As he grew older and more absorbed in his dreams his handling grew rougher and less precise and his loading is pushed to greater and greater extremes. In some of his late work, marvellous as it is in imaginative power, full as it is of humanity and of sympathy, I must confess that the actual painting is, to me, extremely disagreeable.

Just what Dupré gained by his heavy loading it is difficult to see. In comparison with the beautiful fluid touch of Corot or the jewel work of Rousseau his pictures reek of paint. But he is far outdone by some of our moderns, and we have landscapes that look like a bit of studio wall covered with the palette-scrapings of a generation of art students, and arms and legs built out into high relief but looking none the rounder for it—things in which the pigment, instead of being made into a lovely surface, is thrown at us in raw and hideous masses.

Finally, we have a kind of technique invented in our own day—the hatching and dotting of impressionism. It was created for a special purpose, the rendering of the vibration of brilliant light, and so far as it answers its purpose and is applied to subjects appropriate for the display of light for its own sake, it is justified. But the last time I was in the impressionist room of the Luxembourg Gallery it struck me not only that the pictures there were spotty and rough, the surface unpleasant to look at as a surface, but that they did not even give any illusion of light. They were pale, not luminous, and their rough surfaces had caught and held the dust. They were dingy and forlorn; their glory had departed. And across the Seine, in the galleries of the Louvre, were pictures four hundred years old that seemed only the richer and more glowing for the centuries that had passed over them, and pictures older still that looked as fresh and brilliant as if just painted.

Unfortunately, we know too little of the methods of the past to be able to discuss, with any profit, that soundness of workmanship which has kept the panels of Van Eyck fresher than almost anything which has been produced since. We can admire the clear beauty of the color, the exquisite surface, the incredible elaboration of detail which is yet consistent with

a large general effect—we can be sure that
the reputed inventor of oil painting knew
more about the proper use of his materials
than any of his successors—but we do
not know what his materials were nor
how he used them. And we know little
more about the wonderful craftsmanship
of the earlier Italian painters. We can
see that there is a marvellous skill of hand
in the pure, fair modelling and delicate
drawing of Angelico; a miracle of training
in the incisive goldsmith-work of Mantegna; but we have no notion of how we
should go to work to imitate them.

In all good technical methods of painting
there are three things aimed at: soundness
and permanence of workmanship; beauty
of surface; purity and richness of color.
Probably the perfection of primitive technique is forever unrecoverable, and in the
matter of a sound and permanent manner
of painting we can go no farther than to
avoid certain things. We can refuse to use

certain pigments that are notoriously
fugitive; we can avoid mixing certain
colors that chemically affect each other;
we can refrain from repainting until the
under coat of paint is thoroughly dry.
And we can be sure that, other things
being equal, the less paint we have put
upon the canvas the less likelihood there
is of disastrous alterations. But we can
profitably study the æsthetic quality of
the workmanship of various masters and
of various schools, trying to understand
what they thought beautiful in surface
and how they secured fulness of color,
that we may secure as much of these
things as possible in our own work.

And, first, let us consider that bugbear
of the modern painter—hardness. To say
that a picture is hard is of itself sufficient
condemnation in our eyes, yet nothing
seems more certain than that hardness
was, with some of the masters, a virtue
deliberately sought for. Mantegna's draw-

Plate 30.—"The Song of the Shepherd," by Puvis de Chavannes.
Property of the Metropolitan Museum of Art.

ings, made with a pen, are much less precise, much less definite, than the paintings
he made from them. He consciously strove
for a hardness with his brush which his
pen would not give him. And, indeed,
if there is a hardness which is not beautiful it is usually because it is not hard
enough. There is little dignity in the hardness of wood or the hardness of leather
—there is much in the hardness of bronze
or the hardness of crystal. Only if one is
to cast things in bronze or carve them in
basalt, they should be worthy the imper-
ishable material. The hardness of Holbein's wonderful enamel is an essential
and necessary part of its beauty. The
gem-like perfection of line and of composition in Ingres's portraits calls for a
gem-like hardness of execution. If these
things were less hard they could not seem
so permanent—so immortal. The only
reason to fear such hardness as this is
that one has nothing to say which is

worthy of such expression. Such definition is cruel, and exposes the least empti-
ness of thought, the smallest and most
momentary hesitation. It may be well for
most of us to take refuge in a little merci-
ful vagueness; but let us admit this as
a concession to human weakness, not
plume ourselves upon it as on a virtue.

Technical beauty has been attained in
various less strenuous ways, but nearly
all good technical practice has been based
on two considerations: First, that it is
necessary to attend separately to the different elements of painting if any of them
are to be carried to perfection; Second,
that it is necessary to provide, in some
form, for transparency if color is to attain
its highest effectiveness. When a beam of
light falls upon a surface of, let us say,
red paint, some of it is absorbed, and the
red rays predominate in what is reflected
back to the eye, but a great many of the
other rays are also bent back by the re-

sisting surface and the red is confused
with other colors. When a beam of light
traverses a piece of red glass practically
all but the red rays are absorbed and the
eye receives a sensation of pure red. When
paint is laid thinly over an opaque, reflecting surface, the light traverses the
color to the surface below, is reflected
from that, and passes through the pigment
to the eye as if it passed through colored
glass. This is, nearly enough for our purpose, the scientific reason for the use of
transparent color. But there is a separate
reason for the use of the light ground. As
oil paint grows older it tends to darken,
but it also tends to grow more translucent.
If there is a dark ground under it this
translucence intensifies its darkness—if
the ground is light it counteracts it.

Primitive technique provided for the
separate consideration of the elements of
painting, and for the transparency of
color, in the simplest manner. Composi-

tion and drawing were exhaustively studied in the cartoon. This was then traced
upon a perfectly smooth and white surface
with very delicate lines. Light and shade
had hardly to be considered at all. The
various parts of the picture were painted
thinly upon the white ground, each bit
finished before the next was begun, and
when the last bit of the ground was covered the picture was complete. It was
nearly the method of pure water color,
though with a little more use of semi-
opaque pigment, and had all the luminosity and beauty of water color. It is
probably the most permanent method of
painting ever invented, and its only
weakness is its unfitness for full effects
of light and shade. It is apparently the
method employed by Holbein, and it was
revived by the English Pre-Raphaelites.

I do not know who invented what, after
its greatest practitioners, we may call
the Venetian technique, nor when and

how it was developed from the primitive manner. We can only take it, as it was used by the great masters, and try to understand its nature and the reasons for its use. It is especially suited to the expression of full and strong chiaroscuro united with pure and beautiful color, and was practised by Correggio, wherever he got it, as well as by Titian and Tintoretto. In this manner of work the cartoon ceased to be made, and composition, drawing and light and shade were created with the loaded brush upon the canvas, leaving the color to be considered alone, at the end. Of course there was more or less preliminary sketching and drawing, but light and shade had become so important that it modified everything else and the final drawing could not be decided upon without it. This preliminary underpainting was, as nearly as we can tell, practically monochromatic, and was made of little more than black, white and red, Titian using more red while Correggio and Tintoretto used more black and white. It was solid, opaque, and with some graining and roughness of surface, though never excessive in its loading. Over this ground the true color surface was laid thinly, at first in united, transparent washes or glazes, later with modifications of semi-opaque as well as transparent color. The underpainting, in this method, could be worked at as long as necessary, could be reconsidered and modified until design and drawing and light and shade were entirely fused and entirely satisfactory, without danger to the color, which could be given undivided attention when the time came to study it. In this underpainting the modelling of the flesh could be pushed to the utmost degree of refinement, while draperies could be brushed in with the greatest freedom. When it was completed it answered the purpose of the old white ground in giving a cold reflecting surface,

Plate 31.—"Danaë," by Correggio.

In the Borghese Gallery.

over which the color could be laid purely
and sweetly, while its granulation of surface gave crannies for the glazing colors
to lie in or ridges for opaque draggings
to catch upon, thus providing for that
breaking of different colors on the surface
which impressionism has achieved in a
more brutal manner.

In this manner was achieved the glowing
beauty of the earlier canvases of Titian,
the lovely silvery tone of Correggio. It
is, perhaps, the most perfect method of
painting ever invented and has been used
by many painters of different schools,
while other methods have been developed
through modifications of it. Van Dyck
used it in much of his best work, Reynolds
used it, or an attempt at it, and so did
Turner. The delicious pearliness of Vermeer is based upon an underpainting of
black and white or even of blue and white,
so cold is it at times. The only defect of
the method is that it is slow, requiring

long periods of drying, especially if the underpainting is done in oil. In the Venetian work the underpainting was probably done in tempera—a kind of water color—and as the use of tempera declined the purely Venetian manner could not answer the purpose of one who wished to paint much and quickly. Indeed the work of Tintoretto, so much of which is ruinous, shows that it was never a manner which lent itself to hasty production.

For these reasons, that most fecund of painters, Rubens, deeply steeped in the traditions of the great Venetians whom he reverenced, invented a modification of their manner by combining it, to some extent, with the old Flemish primitive method. He used the smooth white ground of the primitives, preferring a panel to a canvas even in large works, and on this ground he laid his monochrome foundation, reducing it to extreme thinness, so that the effect of the ground is everywhere retained and his monochrome is almost more transparent than opaque. Upon this foundation he spread his final painting in great flowing washes of semi-opaque color, dragging in last of all his sharp high lights of loaded pigment. As he grew older and more certainly master of himself and his great stores of knowledge his handling grew ever lighter and swifter, his pigment more tenuous and delicate, until he came to paint almost with vapor, only his high lights having any ponderable substance. To those who are inclined to think thinness of pigment the sign of timidity, and to imagine that heavy loading of paint is a mark of virile strength, the example of this most robust of painters may be recommended for painful consideration.

The Dutch painters of the seventeenth century reduced Rubens's monochrome to a purely transparent rubbing, and painted into it with opaque and semi-opaque pigment. Van Dyck painted in

Rubens's manner when he did not paint in the pure Venetian method. Watteau learned his art of Rubens, and as all the French eighteenth century derives from Watteau and all the English eighteenth century from Van Dyck, the influence of Rubens was predominant in the technique of painting until David swept the whole art away as unregarded rubbish.

It was easier, in considering the development of technical methods, to pass over the work of one of the greatest of technicians who had very little influence on that development, greatly as his work has always been admired by all competent judges of painting. Veronese was never properly a Venetian. He was a mature artist of great reputation before he went to Venice, and he came of a school with a long tradition of its own. Also, he was a decorator, accustomed to canvases of vast size, and to a clearer and lighter key of color than that of the true Venetian school.

I have never seen anything to convince me
that he employed the true Venetian technique, even in the painting of flesh, and
I am sure he did not employ it in the painting of draperies. It is not so easy to say
how he did paint as how he did not, and
in his own handiwork his methods are
used with such discretion and such variety—are so hidden behind the result—
that they seem undecipherable. In the
work of his pupils and assistants, however, the process, or some of it, is more leg-
ible; and we have a written account of it,
lamentably brief, to be sure, based upon
the statement of his son. In the first place
he must have had some sort of pretty
thorough drawing upon his canvas, though
this is not mentioned in the description
we have of his method. I am inclined to
think that it must have been a rub-in, a
frotté, in pretty full light and shade, and
I am sure that it must have fixed all the
important details of the picture. Such

composition as his, extending to the smallest folds of drapery, was never accomplished by leaving anything of importance
to the invention of the moment. Over this
drawing he laid his masses of local color
in half-tone, we are told—these half-tones
being "laid in opaque color." Whether
these masses of half-tone had any modelling I do not know, but if they were laid
pretty thinly and evenly over a strong
frotté, enough of that frotté would show
through them to answer all necessary
purposes. Upon this preparation he struck
in both his lights and his shadows, "leaving the middle tint visible everywhere
between them, as it was first prepared."
In painting in the lights he used a light
yellow rather than white, because yellow
has much greater carrying power and
luminosity than white, and its chromatic
quality, as yellow, is quite lost at a short
distance. The shadows were, undoubtedly,
re-enforced with pure, transparent, glazing

Plate 32.—"Dr. Faustus," from the etching by Rembrandt.

colors. These lights and shadows, with the original middle tint, or local color, between them, are sharply to be distinguished in the work of Veronese's imitators. In his own work they are fused together into the most brilliant, rich and varied surface imaginable. He never makes any display of virtuosity, but for mere ease and accuracy of touch he surpasses the most expert of the Northern painters while his work is vastly superior to theirs in decorative beauty and classic grace.

I have described this manner of painting at considerable length because it seems to me best fitted of any for our modern needs. Indeed it comes pretty near to our modern "direct method" except that it is far more systematic, allowing, as all good methods do, of the separate study of the different elements of the art, and providing for transparency and the breaking of color. The composition, the drawing, and the great masses of light and shade are first fixed in the preliminary frotté. The arrangement of colors and the great color balance of the whole picture are settled in the painting in middle tint. In the final execution there is nothing to think of but the brilliancy of rendering and the quality of color in detail. The transparent re-enforcement of the shadows gives them great fulness and purity of color, while the breaking of the lights, with a crumbly touch, over the middle tints gives the necessary vibration and the necessary graying of surface without any diminution of the force of pure color. It is a method which lends itself admirably to large decorative work which must be done with some rapidity, but I do not see why it is not equally applicable to smaller and more realistic pictures.

Neither here nor elsewhere in this volume, however, am I concerned to give precise recipes, and I can no more tell any one how to paint than how to draw or to color. What I wish to do is rather to call attention to the qualities of art that we have lost sight of in our work of to-day and that we must set ourselves to recover if we would bring painting to anything like its ancient perfection and dignity. Of these qualities craftsmanship is not the least and is one of the most neglected. If I can make you see that technical beauty exists, and that it cannot be attained without thought and method, I shall have fulfilled my purpose.

There have been many good methods of painting—there may, conceivably, be as good methods yet to be invented— but all good methods have these two things in common: they are methodical and they are economical. To paint well, in any manner, one must know from the first touch what the result is to be, and one must place no touch on the canvas that is not a necessary step toward the attainment of this result. Every brush stroke that does not lead to the desired end leads away from it. Every particle of pigment that is not used is worse than wasted, it is obstructive. It is matter out of place, which is the best definition I know of dirt. It may be that the method employed will call for heavy loading, but it must be heavy loading where it is needed and because it is needed. It must be as precisely regulated as the thinnest film of glazing or of scumbling. There is, in good painting, no room for accident and no cure for a blunder. It may be patched, and more or less concealed—it cannot be remedied. To paint well, technically, is to have profound knowledge both of the process and of the result desired; is to have perfect foresight and perfect skill; is to be both craftsman and artist. It is first of all to be a composer, a draughtsman, a colorist, and then, as a crowning grace, to be a technician, a master of one's tools.

And now, if I have at all succeeded in my effort to show what the art of painting is and has been; if I have given any notion of what it means to choose a subject intelligently and treat it largely, nobly, and with imaginative grasp of its significance; what it means to compose a picture thoroughly, so that no detail of it shall escape from the control of the guiding principle of design; what it is to draw with expression, with style, and with precision, and to clothe design and drawing with color at once beautiful and true; what it is, and how difficult, to produce mere material beauty of pigment and of surface—if, I say, I have at all succeeded in this you will begin to suspect that it is no easy road I am pointing out and that it takes more than a cheerful self-confidence, a couple of years in an art school, and a palette and brushes to make a painter. The way of classicism and conservatism is no safe path for the timid and unenterprising, and he who attempts it will find that he will need all, and more than all, the energy, the determination, and the individuality he possesses. He will have to go over and through obstacles, not around them. He will have to hew his way through thickets that have grown up from long neglect. He will have to eschew all tempting by-paths and short cuts. And he will have, for the most part, to go alone, stubbornly holding to his direction while the crowd goes the other way.

What the classic ideal asks of an artist is no less than a thorough mastery of all that is known of the aspects of nature and all that is known of the processes of art, and it requires this merely as a preliminary equipment for creation and for self-expression. The task of acquiring such mastery is almost appalling in its magnitude, but at least there is little danger that he who is capable of an approximation to it will have no personality to express. And there is this encouragement for us, that the thing has been done, and therefore may be done again. It is the failures that are discouraging. When one sees exhibitions and galleries full of pictures, the work of able men who have spent their lives in fruitless effort and have left nothing that will live, one falls into a profound despair of ever doing better than they. But one has only to see one masterpiece—even one bit of honest and beautiful work—and hope revives. If he could do it, why not I? And the greatest masters of all have the divine privilege of making the task seem positively easy.

To the serious young artist I would say: Fix your eye on the highest, gird yourself for the journey, and God speed! If you fall by the way you may at least fall face forward. And it may be that even you may reach the goal. It may be that you, too, may find yourself, in the end, among that small but glorious company whose work the world will cherish and whose memory the world will not let die.

THE SCRIBNER PRESS

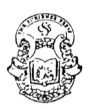

...E OF ART, (Incorp.)

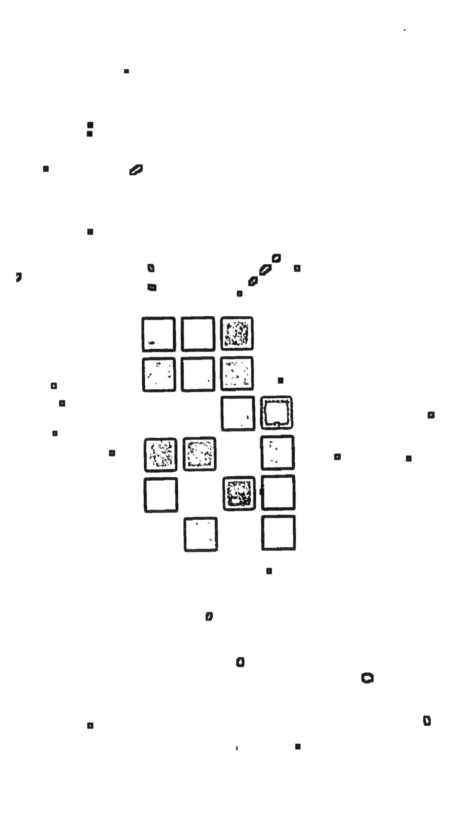

CPSIA information can be obtained
at www.ICGtesting.com
Printed in the USA
LVHW08s1200081018
592787LV00017B/1144/P